ASPIRE AWAKEN
ACTUALISE

ASPIRE AWAKEN ACTUALISE

Journeys to Transformation

MAVIS UREKE

WITH CO-AUTHORS

PARTRIDGE

A Penguin Random House Company

To order additional copies of this book, contact
Toll Free 0800 990 914 (South Africa)
+44 20 3014 3997 (outside South Africa)
orders.africa@partridgepublishing.com

www.partridgepublishing.com/africa

CO-AUTHORS

Mavis Ureke
Stephanie Vermeulen
Jeanne Booth
Ayanda Roji
Shelley Lewin
Shereen Elmie
Svetlana Stankic
Marisia Robus
Diane Collier

Preface: By Mavis Ureke

To The Readers of "Aspire Awaken Actualize"

I have been a trainer and mentor for corporates and individuals who are all on this journey of transformation. In sharing a life picture exercise, which is one of my tools for developing self-awareness, I realized everyone has something to teach about this journey of transformation. Every individual on this journey acquired skills, used tools and techniques that if shared can also help others on their journey. This book series is a toolbox where you can draw out various tools when you need them. The series will give practical tips, tools and techniques as applied by the individual authors on their own journey and also as they assist their clients to transform their lives. It is a collection of experiences from the various authors. For the past decade, I have seen people wanting to change, but stuck, not knowing or not having the tools to assist them in transformation, hence the idea of Aspire, Awaken and Actualize.

As you read this book, you will be exploring practical self-development tools and techniques with proven results. Dr Wayne Dyer said, "all we need is already here, we just need to see it". We have to awaken so we can actualize. Reading this book is like walking the journey of transformation with the authors who are exploring the unlimited possibilities to "Being".

I started this series to bring authors with various expertise together with readers with the various needs. When you read this series it will assist you in the key areas of your life that you may be looking to transform. This is the first book in the series.

The series will embrace each of the following areas:

- Spiritual wellness and well-being
- Physical wellness and well-being
- Relationship Awareness
- Personal Growth and Career attainment of goals
- Parenting children with special needs
- Parenting in the age of transformation
- Values based living
- Financial Wellness
- Dealing with Grief
- And many more areas that require our shift in awareness to the continual journey of transformation

These perspectives come into alignment with Managing Emotions for Success, understanding and leveraging the drivers of behavior to achieve your outcomes. My advice is this work is a **BUY TEN TO SHARE WITH FRIENDS** pledge.

CONTENTS

Living Inside Your Body – The Power of Authenticity

Everyone wants to be something or do something significant, whether that significance is financial success, creativity, relationship success or health and well-being. In trying to achieve this success we all venture into many change or transformation initiatives. Some of them succeed, some only last for a while and others fail. We also expose ourselves to as much information as possible to learn to become better in order to achieve our goals. And as we expose ourselves to this information, we realize what is possible and with increased awareness we begin to aspire to change. Aspiration is the desire for change without the matching action, it involves positive thoughts and sometimes with willpower people may take action to pursue their vision or dream. Some soon get tired of pursuing their goals, while their goals are not yet achieved, or their goals are achieved and they are still not fulfilled. Frustration may build in some people, while others may even become despondent.

I realize that awareness can be externally focused, looking at behaviours, personality and body language or internally focused, looking at thoughts, emotions and sensations. Awareness is what I see about what needs to change and transformation on the other hand is using that awareness so that it becomes how I see it. Transformation is an internal process and this internalization is what creates energy for movement towards the desired change. It is the anchor that moves one from aspiration to inspiration, from an old reality to a new reality. It is not a place we arrive at; it is a continuous journey.

The challenge many of us have is that we have created a static image of ourselves, we get fixated on that image and we refer to it as "WHO I AM".

When you try to change behavior on the outside, the fear of losing the "you that you know" creeps in on the inside and this fear operating from under the radar stops you from taking the necessary action to change or achieve your set goals. As I mentioned, transformation is an internal process that activates the necessary resources or achievement emotions for one to take action.

The question we constantly need to ask when we set our goals is *"What inside of me needs to shift in order to achieve this goal?"*. When we shift inside, behavior on the outside becomes automatic as the anchor has been created inside. The shift occurs when one connects with, expands, establishes guard and influences their identity on a continual basis. This process is selling the idea of change or goal achievement to you. Once you make the sale to yourself, your behavior or action follows. Your identity is made up of values, self-image, traits and motives. Our motives are the essence of humanity therefore similar for everyone, although the way to achieve these motives is not similar. As highlighted by Anthony Robbins, a personal development guru, we have six basic needs or motives, which are certainty, variety, significance, love/connection, contribution and growth. To find fulfillment we continue to change and shift to meet these needs or core motives and this also means a continuous shift in our identity. Our values as part of our identity are the set rules we form on how to meet our core needs.

We are not born with values but develop them through socialisation. Our values are influenced by the emotions we experience when our needs or motives are met or not met at an early age. As such the values formed when your needs are not met may be a defense mechanism, to protect yourself from further pain of not meeting your needs or enabling you to achieve your needs. The values that are protective may also inhibit you from engaging in behaviors that allow you to meet your needs as values drive our behaviors. It is important to note that our emotional states generate values and beliefs unconsciously, hence we may not be consciously aware of these values and yet they drive our behavior.

Sociologist Morris Massey indicated that values form in three periods of our lives. The first period is the imprinting years, which is the age between zero and seven, at the stage when we do not have a mind of our own and we basically absorb everything as true from our parents or caregivers. Then we have the modelling years, between the ages of eight and thirteen, where we copy the values of others and even try them. Our influencers maybe parents, teachers or even religion. We then have the socialization years, between ages thirteen and twenty-one, where we begin to develop our own self-concept by distilling values and aligning ourselves with people who share similar values, however, we are still influenced by the media and our peers. The process of distilling and sieving values has to continue until people can express their unique selves. Expressing your unique self goes beyond socialization and I would like to call this the individuation period. The individuation period is where you go back inside yourself to align the values you learnt from the outside to see which ones fit in. If we do not align these values internally we operate with mass level of awareness where we do things to fit in and to conform to the norms and values of others. It's like owning a house. You have to measure the internal space to determine which size curtains fit, how big your furniture can be, and since it is your property you also have the liberty to expand to ensure that you create what you want it to be. You begin to live from inside your home with peace. However, you cannot do this on rented property. Most of us have rented values and we have given ourselves up to religion, doctors, the government and others. We think others own us, therefore we cannot individuate or customize our values and our internal space. Many fear rejection, loss of relationships, and loss of the known if they individuate. As such decisions are fear-based and externally focused. Questions buzz inside your head "What if the owner of the house comes? What if I fail to pay the rent?" and these questions perpetuate fear. Many people live with conventional values learnt from their parents, teachers and peers.

Perpetual fear is generated by living others' values or projecting your values onto others unconsciously, which is met by resistance from others who have their own values to follow. When you live out your values and continually expand opportunities and options to live your values and consciously finding support for your values, you live with little fear. The fear is not immobilizing, nor is it perpetual fear. This also involves alignment with others' values to live in harmony with others. Many of us assume that if we live in the same house, we share the same values or that our relatives/ spouses should understand and share our values. The truth is they do not always share the same values; hence alignment of values becomes key.

Perpetual fear creates a negative self-belief or false positive belief, which is your self-image. Self-image is internal; it is the true sense of how you feel about yourself, confidence in self-belief, which is not dependent on external value. The way you view yourself is important for goal achievement or transformation. When we do not live out our values or someone or something challenges our values, it can create tension and fear. This creates low self-esteem, which leads in one of two directions. You either blow up, become aggressive, domineering or abusive, to cover up the negativity experienced internally. Alternatively you give up, you shrink within and carry on as if you have nothing to offer. Because a negative self-image continually brings negative emotions to the fore, to escape the unpleasant feelings people find temporary painkillers like addictions, compulsions and obsessions. These can include behaviors, tendencies or substances. The temporary escape offered by these painkillers further stands in your way to live out your values and achieve your goals. Many people have their self-image tied to an event or person that challenged their values. They did not disengage from the situation to go back inside and own their values and live them again. Hence they have created a static self-image and self-belief attached to that event. We have to detach emotionally, mentally and sometimes physically from the event. George Byron, a UK Lord and poet, talking about transformation said, *"I am not now that which I have been"*. We need to create the flexibility to move on and still be aware that we passed through all the places we did. We need to be able to reframe how we see what happened. For example, you can say I went through that, but I am here now. When you reframe you are not resisting what happened, but accepting it in order to change or move past it.

Traits are how we express our unique self through living our values. Living your values gives you an opportunity to own your talents and show your strengths. Traits are not static either. They get better as you continue to dig out your gifts and this is growth. In the areas where you do not live out your values, your weaknesses show or when you have a fear you overemphasize your strengths. The key areas in which we all want to accomplish, include relationships (family and friends), career (purpose and calling), finances, mental, physical or spiritual to fulfill our human needs. Often we live out our values consciously in one of the areas and there our strengths become magnified. In the areas where we do not live out our values, our weaknesses become magnified.

When we do not live out our values and live out those of others, we cannot own our own talents and express our strength, hence we live outside our bodies or we are disconnected from our hearts. Our values reside in our hearts. Your identity, made up of your traits, values, motives and self-image, creates your subconscious mind. You do not have to be consciously aware of a value to live it by either reacting to its infringement through disgust or responding to its support through trust.

Own Your Identity and Continually Transform it

We have been taught to think with our heads, not with our hearts. Hence we begin to use a part of ourselves the cortical brain to set our goals and even to achieve our dreams. As we focus on developing our cortical brain or problem-solving brain, we detach ourselves from our identity. We try to problem solve infringement of our values instead by living them or just being consciously aware of them. And when we focus on using a part of ourselves, we may discover that we are out of alignment. This may result in burnout or struggle to reach our goals or we may even abandon many goals along the way. Our identity is imprinted in our hearts, traits, self-image, motives and the values that reside in the heart and it is the heart that can confirm if your values are your own. It is your emotional states that generates values. We often hear, *"follow your heart"* – this means pursuing your values to meet your human needs – or *"do it from the heart"* – this means tapping into and owning your strengths, gifts and talents – and your self-image is automatically boosted when you connect with your strengths.

Owning your own identity is an internal process, it requires going inside to identity your values and their foundation. It may involve expanding or replacing your values to align them with your vision of yourself, who you want to become, not what you have picked up from others. The process of individuation requires an honest conversation with yourself. It may also be a painful process as it means letting go of things that have carried you for so long, depending on the stage in your life when you have that conversation. This process allows us to connect the brain and the heart so that they work together in harmony. Many people do not want to have this conversation or are not aware that they need to have this conversation. Hence they aspire for better things in their life, but there is no movement. You have to do the inner work to get your mindset, heart and character in alignment. Inner work will help you connect with your creativity, help you create great relationships, financial success, emotional freedom and authenticity.

Transformation occurs when you start being yourself, genuinely, confidently, proudly and with humility. Living out anyone else's values is a waste of the person you are. When you are authentic, as challenges come your way, they do not sway you from pursuing your values. You may be derailed, but you will not be taken off course completely unless you give away your power. As you embrace that individual inside you that has ideas, strengths and beauty like no one else, you become a principled person. Many great leaders were principled; they stuck to their values through various tests and trials. These leaders include Nelson Mandela, Mahatma Gandhi, Mother Teresa, Martin Luther King, to mention a few.

We may not all become icons if we pursue our values, but we will definitely be heroes in our communities and also become our own heroes. When you own your identity you become the person you know yourself to be, you connect with the hero within – the best version of you and you live on your terms. Any perpetual fear is replaced by enthusiasm, new energy and self-love that can not be stolen from you. This is not to say you will not suffer, but you will have internal resources to prepare for, deal with, adapt to and recover from challenges that come your way. Living your values requires discipline at first, as it is a new territory and pattern, and you may find yourself going back to your comfort zone. And remember your trained brain is always telling you to problem solve instead of expanding your options to live out your values. Living your values requires greater inner work and the greatest work you will ever do in this world is self-work, finding those values and crafting an art around living them. To own your identity you have to identify your values in the relationship, financial, career, spiritual and physical domains of your life. You also have to be aware of your self-image built as a result of meeting your needs or not meeting your needs from an early age and the personality that formed as a result.

Ask Questions that Lead You to Your Inner Journey

You may ask, *"How do I start living out my own values? How do I align my values to my goals?"* To own your own identity you have to ask questions that allow you to go back inside to trace and expand your identity. This process of building self-awareness requires self-observation, as some of the questions and answers lie in our behavior – our doing or not doing something. When our needs are not met and we have not figured out how to meet them, we may adopt a coping mechanism. In our coping we form personalities which may be a defense mechanism driven by our emotional states. Many of us have not been educated on how to connect with our emotions or how to release them and to become peaceful before we make a decision. The questions we ask must guide us to the emotions behind the behaviors that are not producing the results we want, as emotions drive our actions and inactions. You cannot have permanent transformation until you really get in touch with your feelings, especially your unconscious impulses and patterns driven by your emotional memory. Your emotions or feelings give you information about whether you are living your values or not. Your feelings will also reveal whether your self-image is true or not, whether you are aligning your values or projecting them onto others or not, and whether your personality is a coping mechanism or authentic.

Transformation is not a place or destination; it is the continuous journey of every living human being. Sometimes the values you have adopted are not aligned to your needs or motives and asking questions may bring that awareness to the fore and you can begin the alignment work. The process of asking questions connects us with our own vulnerability and vulnerability is key to transformation.

Questions are self-focused, not focused on others. Let us explore possible questions to ask to lead us back inside:

➤ What am I feeling as a result of what is happening around me?
➤ Have I felt this before in my life? And if so, what was happening at the time?
➤ What is the earliest age I felt this emotion?
➤ What is the mental story I am telling others or myself because of this feeling?
➤ How do I behave or what do I do when I experience this emotion?
➤ Where am I experiencing this emotion in my body?
➤ Which one of my values is being infringed or challenged by what is going on?
➤ Is my reaction allowing me to live out my value/s?
➤ What is the motive this value is intended to meet?
➤ Is this value enabling me to achieve my goal, or is it defensive and standing in my way to meeting my needs?
➤ Am I projecting my own values onto others?
➤ How can I live out this value?
➤ How am I sabotaging myself from living out my values?
➤ How can I find support for my values?
➤ How can I align my values with others' values?
➤ What other options do I have to live out my values?

Breaking Emotional Patterns

When we question ourselves and get into our inner terrain, we meet with our identity or personality. For some people this will happen for the first time. Meeting your identity consciously can either be interesting or scary. New emotions come up that you also need to be aware of, away from the emotion you may be investigating. Emotional literacy is a key skill in taking the inner journey, but also in breaking emotional patterns. Your identity is expressed through tendencies, impulses and dominant preferred ways of behavior. This expression of identity also signifies your dominant emotional state, or the emotions you could be feeding through your tendencies and behavior.

In order to transform, we have to shift our emotional states and ultimately or automatically our behaviors. When we shift our emotions from fear-based emotions driven by our inability to form values that assist us in meeting our needs or inability to live out our values, to emotions that enable us to live out values and achieve or meet our needs, transformation occurs. Breaking emotional patterns entails creating new emotional patterns from fear-based to achievement-based emotions. We do not have to be victims of our identity, thoughts or emotions, because we can create and continue to recreate all of them. Let us look at a case I dealt with recently, where a client of mine wanted to create a financial shift as she was stuck in debt. We will call her Michelle, although this is not her real name. The debt involved micro-lending with a high interest rate. So we started questioning her to find out what was driving her behavior.

What emotion do you experience as a result of this situation Michelle?
I feel insecure, scared and anxious.

Have you felt these emotions before in your life? And if so, what was happening?
Yes, I was five and nieces who lived in town had come to their rural home in the rural area where we lived. My father and mother did not work, so we did not have much. While we were playing my nieces mentioned how we could not afford chicken for Christmas, as we had nothing. I felt small, invisible, insignificant and insecure.

This may not always show up easily. It may require tracing your life story to get in touch with some of your emotional experiences that may be creating your behavior patterns.

How old were you?

I was five years old.

What mental story do you tell yourself because of this feeling?

I tell myself that I am unworthy, that I am not good enough and will never be significant.

How do you behave or what do you do when you experience this emotion?

I create emergencies so that I borrow money to feel secure for a moment. So I basically try to run away from this emotion by problem solving it. I am also very cautious, hence I do not trust easily. I always feel people are out to get me or minimize me.

Where do you experience this emotion in your body?

I feel the insecurity just below my rib cage on both sides. It is a horrible feeling.

Which one of your values is being infringed or challenged by what is going on?

My financial value is financial freedom, with little or no debt. So when I borrow it increases my insecurity, anxiety and fear.

Is your reaction allowing you to live out your value/s?

Not at all. When I borrow to feel secure temporarily, I move away from living out my financial value.

What is the motive this value is intended to meet?

The motives for financial freedom are significance, certainty, comfort, security, contribution and connection.

Is this value enabling you to achieve your goal or is it defensive, hence standing in your way to meeting your needs?

The value helps me to achieve financial freedom if I live it out. However, financial freedom can be expanded to mean creating internal stability that is not swayed by my financial state, which is outward and creating enough security for me internally. Thank you for this process as it is allows me to see this clearly. My need for security does not only have to be tied to my bank balance, but also to the relationships I create across the key areas of my life.

Are you projecting your own values onto others?

Yes, when I borrow I become resentful of people that lend me money as I am feeling the negativity of not living out my value system.

How can you live out this value?

As I mentioned earlier, I can live out this value by expanding the meaning of financial freedom, create security across key areas of my life.

How have you been sabotaging yourself from living your values?

By running away from the feeling, creating emergencies to borrow money and in the process missing out on opportunities to either get support from family and friends I have been sabotaging myself.

How can you find support for your values?

The initial support is the one I will give myself. I realize I have carried insecurity in my body for over 30 years and I choose to let it go. It may take time, but now I am aware of it so I see it rising. Instead of jumping out of my body to run away from that emotional experience, I will allow it to come through, and observe without acting on it. I will also observe it with compassion. I was five years old then, I felt trapped, but I am thirty-six now and I have the power to create the life I want without the limitation of false insecurity. And I have realized that I have actually achieved a lot of significant things and I will persevere to build internal security. I will ask and accept help when I need it. I will communicate my values more. I will also find an accountability buddy who watches out for my tendencies and keeps me on track or helps me to expand my options.

How can you align your values with others' values?

I will communicate my values more and learn what other people's values are and endeavor to find common ground.

What other options do you have to live out your values?

I will learn more about money to create awareness and clarity so that I can start investing my way to financial freedom on the outside as well. I will expand my product base to offer more products to the market while keeping an eye on the emotional patterns that drive my financial patterns. I also realize that I am more creative when I am stress free and not feeling insecure.

I have summarized the answers to this process. This process moves one from looking at the surface level of the behavior that needs to change to the drivers of behavior. This reprograms and breaks the limiting emotional memory and pattern by creating mind and emotion awareness and creating that internal connection and transformation. This allows your authenticity to show through instead of being manipulated by emotional patterns that may be as old as you are while you are unaware of them. And as we go through life, we will become stuck again and again, but we need to keep transforming.

Enjoy your transformation journey!!

Mavis Ureke, MA

Mavis Mazhura is an author, public speaker and corporate trainer for the past 6 years. She is an authorized and official certified SDI facilitator of Personal Strength South Africa in applying Relationship awareness in life, certified Emotional Intelligence, Critical Conversations, Personal Energy Management, Creativity and Innovation Trainer. She is also a certified John Maxwell Leadership Trainer and Coach. Her passion is equipping and empowering individuals to expand human awareness and reach their full potential. She has one on one and group coaching programmes. Mavis has trained from lower to board level management teams in Uganda, Botswana, South Africa, Zimbabwe and Namibia. Mavis specializes in Human Behaviour and Human Factor Programmes. She is the author of Navigating the Rapids and the Waves of Life: Managing Emotions for Success: 10 Lessons for Managing Emotions for Success. Mavis Mazhura is a Human Behaviour Specialist and the cofounder of Training B2B CC, a training company based in Johannesburg, South Africa. Contacts: Training B2B CC Tel: +27 11 326 2499 website: www.mavisureke.com email: mavism@ tb2b.co.za

Three keys for creating empowering mindset aligned with the abundance, happiness and success you desire!

There is much talk these days about limiting beliefs. But what exactly is a limiting belief? Simply put, a limiting belief is something that gets in the way and keeps you from living the life of your dreams. My purpose here is to help you better understand what keeps you from achieving the success, prosperity, happiness, and peace of mind you want—what you can do to create permanent positive changes and attract more of what you want to experience into your life. I will guide you through some simple, yet powerful exercises to help you to learn:

- how to uncover limiting beliefs that run in your subconscious mind;
- how you can release and free yourself of limiting beliefs; and
- how you can transform limiting beliefs into an empowering mindset aligned with what you want to experience.

What are limiting beliefs and how do they rule our life?

According to Tony Robbins, a belief is a feeling of certainty about something. For example, if you believe that you're intelligent, all you're really saying is, "I feel certain that I'm intelligent."

The story of a circus elephant is a helpful metaphor in understanding limiting beliefs. As an infant, the elephant was tied securely by a rope to a pole and could move no further than the length of rope allowed. As the elephant grew bigger and stronger, it could easily snap the rope or pull the pole out of the ground to free itself, but it stopped trying. The elephant developed the belief that it could not set itself free.

How many of us are like this circus elephant? Give up on ourselves because of past failures? Hold ourselves back or not even try because of outdated beliefs on what is possible? How many of us have adopted an "elephant mentality" rooted in limiting beliefs of our childhood we were taught by our parents, our teachers, and other authorities? As time goes by and our experiences accumulate, we begin to simply abide by our restrictions without so much as questioning them. Years later we continue to believe that we are incapable of expanding our boundaries.

Ninety percent of our success derives from our mindset and divine guidance. Changing these two elements will transform our life!

Mindset is defined variously as "a fixed mental attitude or disposition that predetermines a person's responses to and interpretations of situations" *(The Free Dictionary)* or "the established set of attitudes held by someone" *(Oxford Dictionary)*. Simply stated, our mindset is our way of thinking.

To understand the role of our mindset in determining our success in life, it is helpful to view mindset from the perspective of the "law of attraction" equation:

Thought + Feeling + Action = Outcome

When we have a belief, a *thought*, it triggers an internal emotional charge, a *feeling*. Our feeling determines our response in a certain situation—an *action* we might take or not take. Our combined thoughts, feelings, and actions in a given situation result in a certain *outcome*.

As Jim Rohn says, "Your attitude determines your altitude."

Ninety-five percent of our actions, beliefs, and feelings are controlled automatically by our subconscious mind!

What is needed to create positive life changes?

To create positive life changes, and be able to act on the Guidance you are given, it is extremely important to align your thoughts, emotions and actions with your goals. This will place you into a higher energy-vibration frequency that will attract the success you desire. More than all other types of resources, it is your beliefs that determine your success in life.

Some limiting beliefs may be conscious—things you tell yourself that block or stop you. For example, when you say, "I want to start my own business, but I am hesitant," you are aware of a limitation and can change it consciously. Other limiting beliefs are like programs running in the background of your mind and can make it impossible for you to get where or what you want despite all the efforts you take. For example, say you want to earn $10,000 per month, but for some reason you never seem to get there. Perhaps when you were six years old, you were bullied by a rich boy and subconsciously decided to be nice. At that time, you established a belief that you cannot be nice and be rich at the same time. This belief served you at some level then by protecting you. But now, you do not need this belief of a six-year-old; it limits and restricts you—just as the rope tied to the pole limits and restricts the grown elephant.

If your thoughts are "I'm afraid I can't do it" or "What if I fail?", your feelings will be of fear. Being afraid of failure, you will procrastinate or allow opportunities to pass you by. When the outcomes you want seem to elude you and you struggle to reach your goals, then one or more parts of the "success formula" may be out of alignment. Ask yourself, "Is my mindset aligned with my objectives?" You need to release the limitations of your mindset and open yourself to your divine guidance to create a mindset of abundance aligned with your heart and soul.

Three keys to create positive life changes

It is obvious to us that the circus elephant of the story could break free and go wherever it desires—but it is not at all obvious to the elephant. If the elephant were to become aware of its size, strength, power, and other abilities, the elephant could easily change his situation.

First key: Awareness of limiting beliefs
As soon as you become aware of what you need to change in your life, change has already started to happen.

> *When we understand what beliefs hold us back*
> *and transform them into an empowering mindset,*
> *we can take our life to a whole new level!*

Here is an exercise that will help you to develop your self-awareness and identify your limiting beliefs. This exercise can be applied to any area of life since your same limiting beliefs tend to surface in different forms in all areas of life. The good news is that once you identify and transform a limiting belief in one area of life, all the other areas of life also benefit.

Get out a pen and some paper, and find yourself a place where you can sit comfortably and there are a minimum of distractions. Choose one of the following areas of life that most affects you now. Take a few minutes to reflect on the area in which you feel most challenged and want to achieve specific and tangible results.

- Money and finances
- Business and career
- Love and relationships
- Health and weight-loss

STEP 1. Think of one specific result that you want to achieve in this area and write it down. For example:

I want to make $10,000 per month.
I want to weigh 63 kg.

STEP 2. Now, write:

I can't achieve this because …

Be totally honest with yourself and dig deep within yourself for reasons. If you do, you will discover core limiting beliefs that are at the root of you as a person. Write down at least five or six reasons why you could not achieve your goal. For example:

- *It will make me less spiritual.*
- *It is too stressful.*
- *I am not pretty enough.*
- *I am not smart enough.*
- *I have to have money in order to make money.*
- *I have already tried everything and nothing worked.*

The more often you repeat this step, the more new reasons you are likely to discover.

What you write down are your **conscious** limiting beliefs which are holding you back. They are the symptoms of your hidden **subconscious** limiting beliefs. All subconscious limiting beliefs fall into a few general categories:

- Fear of failure: *If I try, I am going to fail.*
- Fear of success: *If I try, I may succeed.*
- *No one will want me. / I am not lovable.*
- *I am not worthy. / I am not deserving.*
- *I am not capable.*

STEP 3. Place your conscious limiting beliefs in the appropriate category of subconscious limiting beliefs. For example:

- Fear of failure: *If I try, I am going to fail.*

  No one has shown me. I don't have enough experience. I don't have good role models. I am too old now. I don't have the money, time, or energy. I have tried everything and nothing worked. The economy is bad. Making money takes too much effort.

- Fear of success: *If I try, I may succeed.*

  There is too much stress associated with money. I can't say no to people. There is always something more important to take care of first. People who look out for themselves first are selfish. When things seem to be going well for me, I get afraid something will happen to ruin everything.

- *No one will want me. / I am not lovable.*

  I am not good enough. People will be jealous and hate me. My family wouldn't approve. I am destined to be alone. I am not pretty enough.

- *I am not worthy. / I am not deserving.*

  It is selfish of me to want more; I should be happy with what I have. I do not deserve it. It is meant for others and not for me.

- *I am not capable.*

  I don't know how. I am not smart or educated enough. It is not something I'm good at. I won't be able to follow through.

Congratulations! You have just identified your dominant subconscious limiting beliefs in one area of life. All of the reasons you listed fall into one or more—possibly even all—of these categories. And very likely these subconscious limiting beliefs affect in different forms many or all areas of life other than the one on which you focused. Good news is that if you change these subconscious limiting beliefs, you will improve not this area but all other areas of your life, too.

Now that you are aware of and have identified a few of your limiting beliefs, you are ready to get to work on releasing these limiting patterns and transforming them into empowering beliefs.

Second key: Releasing limiting beliefs

To release a limiting belief, it is helpful for you to clear your feelings associated with the belief. Let's explore some ways to achieve this.

Choose one of the limiting beliefs from your list:

Think of your feelings associated with this limiting belief. Find the place in your body where you feel them. What colour do you associate with these feelings?

Now, think of a time in your life when everything was okay for you. What colour do you associate with these feelings?

Take a deep breath.

As you exhale, sense the energy in the colour of the feelings associated with the limiting belief leaving you until you notice how these feelings are finally all outside of you. Notice the change in energy as this feeling-bad colour changes into the feeling-good colour of when everything was okay and say to yourself, "It's all changed now."

As you inhale, sense the new energy of the feeling-good colour entering you and say to yourself, "It is all in me now". Imagine this energy filling you up completely from head to toe, permeating every cell of your body.

An alternative exercise that you can use to release your limiting belief is to visualize the limiting belief as an object. Imagine yourself throwing the object into a fire and watching it burn to ashes. Or, write the limiting belief on a chalkboard and watch it slowly fade until it is entirely erased. Or, observe the limiting belief flying away until it disappears on the horizon. Every time, say to yourself, *"It's gone. I'm free now."*

Remind yourself that you can always feel like this whenever you want. And remember that you can change how you feel any time you want.

This powerful exercise can be applied to every limiting belief on your list. Practise a few times every day for six weeks—each time you catch yourself responding from your limiting conditioned fearful, doubtful, low-esteem, joyless mindset instead of from the divinely guided abundant mindset of your heart and soul.

Third key: Reprogramming limiting beliefs into an empowering mindset

Let's explore a few different practices and tools that can help you to reprogram your limiting beliefs into an empowering mindset.

Affirmations. One very powerful way to improve your view of yourself and change your limiting beliefs and attitudes is daily practice of positive affirmations. Here are some examples of affirmations you can use. Choose one or more that appeal to you and are appropriate to your situation, or make up your own.

- *I am strong.*
- *I am happy.*
- *I am love.*
- *I am creative.*
- *I am in charge of my life.*
- *I am well organized.*
- *I am confident.*
- *I am creative.*
- *I am unique.*
- *I am loved.*
- *I am safe.*
- *I am prosperous.*
- *Only good things happen to me.*

To get the most out of your affirmations, say them out loud to yourself at least once every day for three months. With time, you will reprogram your outlook and start to attune yourself to higher energy vibration and more positive thinking. You will transform yourself to better reflect your true inner radiant nature.

Clearing feelings. A more direct way to create a mindset change is to work on clearing feelings around thoughts and beliefs. The goal of this exercise is to help you to change your typical state of consciousness that governs your personal perceptions and experiences. An adaptation of a process developed by Gregory Downey, the exercise works on feelings that are expressions of your conditioned self that are controlled by your limiting beliefs—feelings such as fear, anger, shame, guilt, worry, inadequacy, spite, envy, sadness, rejection, desperation, hopelessness, helplessness.

The procedure is very simple: Check in with yourself at regular intervals at least ten times during the day. As a reminder, tie a thread around your wrist, post sticky notes, or set the alarm on your i-Phone. Every time you are prompted, ask yourself, *"How do I feel right now?"*

If how you feel is positive, say to yourself, *"Thank you for checking in. I love you, I love you, I love you."*

If there is any negativity to how you feel, identify it as false and remind yourself that it is only your interpretation of the experience and simply "an old program" running. Say to yourself, ***"There it is, that's not me, that's a program."*** Notice what physical and emotional sensations you feel and locate where you feel them. Define the sensations and their location simply, saying to yourself, ***"It feels like (this). I feel it (here)."*** **This places you in the role of observer and helps you to detach from the experience. Then, say to yourself,** ***"Thank you. I love you, I love you, I love you."*** Thank yourself for no longer feeding the program, for unlearning the falsehood and relearning the truth. Thank yourself for catching yourself and no longer losing energy here. *"I love you, I love you, I love you."*

Or, in brief:

- ***There it is, that's not me, that's a program.***
- ***It feels like (this). I feel it (here).***
- ***Thank you. I love you, I love you, I love you.***

Perform this 15-second exercise every time you sense a negative emotion. It is not intended to help you get rid of your negative feelings, but to change your conditioned responses to new conscious responses. In time, these new conscious responses will become your habitual responses.

Building self-confidence. Boosting self-confidence and raising feelings of self-worth helps you to change your emotional state related to core beliefs about your false self-image. This helps you to release limiting beliefs and change them with empowering trust in your self-worth, thus developing an empowering mindset. Here is an exercise adapted from a guided meditation of Adam Mortimer that you can use to build and improve your feelings of self-confidence.

Imagine yourself a year into the future. Project yourself as if you are in a place where you have already achieved what you want. See yourself doing the job of your desires, running your own business, writing a book, being in top form and perfect health, enjoying a loving relationship, closing a lucrative deal ...

Now, think of the colour that represents confidence to you. While you are in this place in the future, imagine how a ball of light of this colour fills you inside. See how the ball of light in this wonderful colour of confidence begins to grow and become brighter and stronger to the point that the colour fills your entire aura. In your mind, paint this place in the future with this colour of confidence.

Observe the empowering feelings that this colour of confidence gives you—the feelings of confidence you already have and carry inside you. Remember these empowering feelings. Project this colour of confidence to whatever you want to achieve in the future.

Energy healing. Energy healing is a powerful catalyst of change. As well as a tool to clear and recharge energy field, energy healing is a way to transform limiting beliefs into empowering beliefs.

A cutting-edge technique called Advanced Pulse˚ developed by Jo Dunning is especially effective in helping to bring about personal change. This technique targets limiting beliefs and feelings around them at the core of unwanted experiences. Clearing deeply rooted limiting beliefs promotes shifts in our thought patterns and perceptions and at the same time raises the vibrancy of our energy field.

The technique helps not only to create changes that a person would like to see in their life, but also to bring into life more of the things that the person wants to experience, to have, or to become. It also promotes changes in outlook and understanding of life, so a person feels more positive and happier as well as more "in the flow" and "connected." In time, things that once were issues become of lesser concern or eventually disappear.

Through energy healing, a person develops and strengthens abilities to perceive options and to act by choice—instead of simply reacting to circumstances over which the person feels no control. This repositions the person from being "a victim" to being "in charge." Challenges and what the person considered "mistakes" once, become lessons in life and opportunities for growth and learning.

> *When we learn what rules our life,*
> *we develop an empowering mindset and*
> *we place ourselves in command of our life.*

Greatness is within you!

My goal was to introduce you to some practices, exercises, and tools to help and inspire you to create an empowering mindest aligned with all of the abundance, happiness, and success you desire.

You have learned three keys to creating a positive change in your life:

- Identify your limiting beliefs
- Release your limiting beliefs
- Create an empowering mindset

You can master your limiting beliefs and develop an empowering mindset. Once you are free of what holds you back, you can move forward with ease as well as attract, create, and manifest more of what you would like to experience.

Now, you are ready to take your life to a whole new level!

Svetlana Stankic

Svetlana is an energy healer, holistic mentor, and poet who helps individuals to unleash their creativity, inspiration and imagination, and to heal through spiritual and energetic practices so that they can live an abundant life of purpose while sharing their gifts with the world.

She is a **Certified Quantum-Touch® Instructor, Reiki Master, Quick Pulse®, Certified Advance Pulse® and Rolodex® Practitioner, Reconnection® & Reconnective® Healing Practitioner,** and a **Deeksha / Oneness Blessing Giver.** Svetlana is a published poet and blogger as well.

Svetlana works with clients across the globe from her home base in Toronto.

For more information, visit: www.NewZest4Life.com or email: Svetlana@NewZest4Life.com.

The Awareness of Birth

The "unborn child is a feeling, remembering, aware being, and because he is, what happens to him – what happens to all of us – in the nine months between conception and birth moulds and shapes personality, drives and ambitions in very important ways"
    – The secret of the unborn child – Dr Thomas Verny with John Kelly

Birth is a unique moment for every one of us: a moment that defines each of us as an individual although we all pass through the same stages from being enclosed and contained to expansion and openness. Yet for each one of us the journey is unique. We take our first breath.

'To be born means to be able to breathe, to embark on that perpetual motion that will be with us till we die'. (Frederick Leboyer)

To live freely we need to breathe freely, with full expansion not only of our lungs but of all of who we are, fully expressed and abounding with Grace and Love.

Most of us do not remember being born, and yet our birth experience has probably been one of the most significant events to impact on our lives. It determines how we view ourselves and how we feel about being alive in this world. The formative period of our lives, the nine months in utero and the first six years of childhood, is the time when we form the decisions about ourselves that define our lives.

"We share an understanding that within each cell of our bodies, we carry an imprint from our formative period." Elena Tonetti-Vladimirova – Birth into Being

Thankfully there is an enormous amount of research being done on the relationship between the mother's experiences during pregnancy and birth and the effects these have on the child. These experiences may determine how we feel about being alive, and shape our learning capabilities, as well as shape how we function as adults and within relationships – whether we feel supported and safe in our space in the world.

For centuries there have been old wives tales about what you eat, think, and pray about having an influence on the nature of your child. In some cultures this influence was used to enable the mother to deliver a healthy boy child to continue the family line. What if there was an essence of truth in this belief? The possibility that we can consciously influence our children and their children becomes an exciting and liberating concept. The eggs that will form our grandchildren are formed in our developing daughters in our wombs. We have a potential gift for sending love, acceptance and positive intelligence down the line of generations.

I believe that we can and do have a direct line to our unborn children. We can become conscious engineers in the planning and dreaming of our children and then, once they are conceived, we can have a very vital and important role to play in their developing bodies, minds and emotions. The unborn developing baby is constantly tuned in to the mother's every emotion, movement and thought. Conscious conception, pregnancy and birth lay the foundations for our children and the future generations to come.

"We have entered an era in which scientific studies have validated that mind and body are interconnected and interdependent" (The Language of Fertility by Niravi B. Payne, M.S.)

In the past we thought that the mind and brain were totally separated from the body. Now we know that what we think and how we feel have a direct impact and consequence on our physical body. How we feel and think about ourselves and our world, both past and future, directly impacts on how our body responds. In the world of conscious fertility this means that pregnancy and birthing give us as parents, enormous scope to influence the development of our children. 'A twinkle in your father's eye' reminds us of the premise that we may exist as a thought before we come into physical incarnation. By raising awareness and consciousness about the process of becoming parents we open up a whole new paradigm for bringing children into this world.

I believe that being a parent is truly a Spiritual Act. It is the Action that I daily take on as what I Believe about myself will lead to how I Act and respond. This is the beauty of being a Conscious Parent. It has nothing to do with how I talk to my child, the foods I ate when I was pregnant, or whether I had a natural birth or elective caesarean. It is my daily journey with myself that then radiates out and enfolds my children, my partner and my world.

I understand there to be many powerful ways of Being as a pregnant woman. However, there is much work to be done within the birthing field. In the medical field pregnancy is often treated as a medical condition rather than a natural process. There are situations in which medical intervention is a necessity but in spite of this, many mothers in this situation consciously choose and strive to bring healthy, loved children into their world. Unfortunately, in some hospitals the medical intervention and birth care are abysmal. This negatively impacts baby and mother bonding and can lead to problems in the mother's parenting skills and the baby's development. Elena Tonetti-Vladimirova calls this lack of awareness and information our 'weakest link'. Until we can consciously shift the standard of maternal and birth care we are stuck in a self-perpetuating destructive loop. Recent research in neuroscience shows that breaking this destructive loop would open many developmental possibilities that transform individuals in their roles as wives/husbands, lovers and parents. With more technical pregnancies happening – IVF (in vitro fertilization), artificial insemination, surrogacy - I think we owe it to the future of our planet and the human race to be as conscious and aware as possible of our thoughts, actions and decisions about bringing children into this world.

If we are going to make the world a more beautiful place, with better leadership, solutions,

And higher quality of human existence,

It needs to start with the seeds we plant into our lives, bodies, our every thought, now.

Our future is determined by the choices we make this moment.

Our conception begins by connecting the soul to the body to ignite our creative potential

So we can confidently lead our children to theirs.

Elizabeth Manning

We daily make decisions that can impact and affect our children for the rest of their lives. This process begins before we conceive. Some of the research I do pertaining to couples who are struggling to fall pregnant shows that they are driven by how they were parented. Often the failure to conceive is due to an unconscious belief, or a forgotten or traumatic experience. When we bring that to the surface and they have an opportunity to work with, clear and forgive those aspects of themselves or others, the block to conception falls away and they are able to sustain a healthy and powerful pregnancy and birth process. Also, the template by which they lived their lives can then be rewritten.

The Question of Consciousness

We are entering an age where we have access to far more information than ever before. When I look back at my experience of being a mother – firstly as a single mom 25 years ago and now as a mom of 2 within a loving and caring relationship – I am aware of two very different scenarios. I love what Bruce Lipton says: 'One cannot be 'guilty' of being a poor parent unless one is already aware of this information and disregards it". I am a very different person now and so my parenting is very different. My plans for birthing my later babies were more conscious and were determined by what I thought was the better birthing option both for them and for me, as well as taking my husband into account. In addition, because my circumstances had changed so did my parenting skills. I treated each of my children differently even though they were only 18 months apart. We are not the same parent to each of our children. Why? Because we are not the same people. We change, grow and evolve.

We've learnt along the way. Our challenge is to take this learning deeper and make it more conscious.

How can we consciously and effectively create the most potential for our unborn children? According to Bruce Lipton, our genes create our potential: they are not necessarily our destiny. This implies that we have the ability to change our destiny, to change our lives. We can and do have the ability to make different and empowered choices about how we conceive and raise our children. Choosing to create a baby can become a Spiritual Act - an act of God/ the Universe/ the Creator/ Spirit. By Spiritual I mean that it is a conscious thought that is filled with love. Creating a child becomes an act of Love in every essence of the word.

In some cultures when a couple decides to have a family there is a process of mental and physical cleansing, healing and preparation. This purification ritual leads the couple to a space of consciousness and awareness in preparation for their journey of becoming parents. They seek guidance from their elders and leaders. The wellness and continuation of the tribe depends on this. We have access to 'magic' now in many forms of technology, information, and tools with which to support ourselves through a journey of preparation for becoming parents. Even through the process of IVF (in vitro fertilization where the egg is fertilized externally and then the embryo is implanted into the uterus) one can work with the energy of conscious creation every step of the way, inviting the spirit of the unborn child into our lives.

As we enter into the journey of self-awareness, of how we feel about becoming parents, and work through the aspects of our own birth including our relationship with our parents during our mother's pregnancy, we bring about the choices that lead to transformation. We have access to processes for clearing and healing painful memories, which in turn gives us the opportunity to choose something different for our lives and our children.

My experience is that starting a process of physical and emotional clearing before conception is a powerful tool to bring both potential parents onto the same page, and to give them an opportunity to clear their past experiences. Many couples that I work with when asked about how they feel about becoming parents give answers that surprise their partners. Taking the time to be honest about how you remember your upbringing and sharing these experiences with your partner is a powerful start to making sure that you are able to work together as a parenting unit. This does not mean that you have to agree on everything, and believe me, there will be times when you disagree. It is easier to be mutually supportive and to create a supportive and caring platform for discussion and healing if you are aware of each other's experiences, and the origin of your own patterns. If you are adoptive parents it helps to be aware that the child is also unconsciously influenced by their biological parents' input. The feelings of rejection and being unwanted may lie deep in their unconscious programming and it may be an issue that you might choose to work with very consciously and constructively.

In her book, Being Born, Robyn Fernance poses a very interesting theory of how our actual birth experience may affect our learning and emotional skills. For example, if the baby is overdue and then has a prolonged labour due to being induced, and this in turn leads to complicated medical intervention, the stress of the mother and baby could give rise in the long term, to the child feeling needy, afraid of having to do things themselves, always needing help, feeling the world is an unsafe space, and that pleasure turns to pain. Then when the child becomes an adult they might feel afraid of relationships because they always end disastrously, and/or they might feel unsupported and always rushed, that they cannot do things in their own time. Currently, there is research being done on the connection between teen violence and the teenagers' experience as newborns in their first few months of birth. James W. Prescott, Ph.D has written many articles on how deprivation of physical touch and affection leads to violence, aggression, depression and drug abuse. Separating the baby from the mother for extended periods of time may have long lasting effects on the child's ability to have healthy and sustainable relationships later on in life. So what to do if this was your experience growing up? All is not lost! There are methods and therapists that can support you in healing your wounded inner child. It is imperative that you find a therapist and therapy that you can relate to as these issues are often deep and complicated, and to ensure that you work with an experienced therapist who is able to support you through your process.

We need to encourage awareness in hospitals and among birth care professionals of the importance of maternal/infant bonding and breastfeeding. If there is a medical reason that the mother and baby need to be separated then bringing the partner on board is absolutely essential and can help to support this bonding process. A conscious step in this direction would be to ensure that the health care professionals whose services you use are in alignment with your choices. You do not want to be fighting with nursing staff when trying to bond with your new born baby.

My personal Journey – a case study

The exciting part about awareness of our birth process is what we can do about it and the change this can bring to our whole life. In this way awareness leads to transformation on a practical level. Through reclaiming the energy that is held in our body we release it to flow more freely. This in turn allows us to do and be and choose things differently not only for ourselves but also for our children.

When I started to work with my birth process, I discovered a host of information about myself that led me on a fascinating journey. When I asked my mum about it she said that it was totally normal and that when she held me in her arms, she forgot everything and she felt that no other woman had been able to do what she had done. She was so proud of herself. That sounded promising.

When I started to ask her for specific details I found it had been a long labour. I was her first baby and she really was a very naive new mum: she did not have a clue what was happening to her body nor did she know what to expect. She was alone in a ward and attended by two nurses who were not very forth coming or supportive. Every time she wanted to move or get up with the labour pains – following her intuition and body messages - she was told to stop being naughty and to lie down. A couple of times they held her down. She found this very hard, difficult, and painful, and became stressed and anxious. She was anxious to please and yet unable to follow her body's process. I was born flooded with these emotions and anxieties. This was my introduction to the new world. Held upside down and slapped to make me breathe properly and then taken away from my mother to be cleaned and washed while she rested and recovered from the birth. I was held in a nursery with bright lights and monitors and brought to her on a trolley every 4 hours on a strict regime to be fed. Being picked up when I cried was frowned on as it was regarded as spoiling.

When I heard this so many things fell into place. I started to understand the way in which I had been unconsciously reacting to situations in my world. I discovered aspects about my personality that kept repeating themselves and over which I seemed to have no control. No matter how much I tried to 'rebel' it would lead me to feeling anxious and uncomfortable. Allowing my instincts to lead me did not feel natural and would bring up internal conflict. I found it difficult to make decisions that would suit me and was happy to compromise myself to suit others. Now I had something to work with. This awareness of my subconscious personality programming enabled me to be gentle and forgiving with myself and gave me an opportunity to choose something different.

An exercise for Birth Change:

Find out about your own birth. How did your mother feel about being pregnant with you? What was her relationship with your father like? Was it a 'difficult' pregnancy? Try to gather as much information as you can. Chat to friends that knew your parents at the time – you might be surprised with the information they can share. So much of this information can give you insight into how you view the world, and that will give you have some tools with which to begin the work of getting to know your unconscious reactions and programmes.

Jeanne Booth

A quote above my desk pulls me forward every day – "I don't want to die with my music still in me"….. and right now there's a lot of music.

My passion and focus is to support women into feeling empowered and connected with their bodies. I love my work. I realise now that the puzzle pieces of my life have all combined to support me into a deeper compassion and understanding of the women I work with and provide me with deeper insights into how I can walk with them on their journey. Combined with the private practice I also run retreats, the latest of which is THE GATHERING co-facilitated with my husband Linden an Executive Flow Coach and EFT Master Facilitator Bennie Naude.

Jeanne is a qualified Fertility Coach, Advanced EFT, Matrix Reimprinting and Matrix Birth Reimprinting practitioner. She combines various modalities such as Massage and Aromatherapy, Reflexology, Cranio-Sacral Therapy, Energy Healing (including Flower Remedies, Reiki, Holistic Body Balance, and visualizations) to support your body to relax, integrate and reconnect with your own innate inner healing and wisdom

She is a doula and works with pregnant women, women with fertility issues, and offers support for IVF and Assisted Reproductive Technology (ART). She is also currently writing a book about Conscious Conception and the Journey to empowered Fertility

Helpful references:

www.jeannebooth.com

http://www.birthintobeing.com
- workshops and information by Elena Tonetti-Vladimirova
http://www.magicalnewbeginnings.com/matrix-birth-reimprinting/
www.matrixreimprinting.com
www.violence.de
articles by James W. Prescott Ph.D

Frederick Leboyer, 1974, Birth without Violence
Bruce Lipton, 2005, Biology of Belief
Niravi B. Payne, 1997, The Language of Fertility
Robyn Fernance, 2003, Being Born
Dr Thomas Verny with John Kelly, 1981, The Secret life of the Unborn child –
Suzanne Arms, 1994, Immaculate Deception
Michel Odent, 1984, Birth Reborn
James Swartz, 2008, The Mind-Body Fertility Connection

ADD/ADHD:
A blessing in disguise

Whenmy child was diagnosed with the "dreaded disorder", I was in shock and started reading everything I could find on the subject. As with so many things in life, there was some helpful information and some that, in my opinion, was inappropriate and confusing. As the human behaviour expert, Dr John Demartini teaches: "Every situation has an equal amount of benefits and drawbacks" and the moment you realise that, life with ADD/ADHD, and life in general, becomes a whole lot easier.

As a parent of a child with ADD/ADHD you will be faced with many choices in your life, and you will make some good and some bad choices. The main thing is to remember that your child is special, and not in the negative sense of the word but the definition: *better, greater, or otherwise different from what is usual.*

FIND THE BENEFITS

This is probably the most important realisation you need to come to, as early as possible. Once you have mastered the understanding of "special", ADD/ADHD will no longer be such a huge issue in your life.

Every human being possesses all 4 600 character traits, as listed in the Oxford Dictionary. Half of them is good or positive and the other half is bad or negative. You will sometimes be kind and sometimes nasty, friendly and grumpy, rude and polite. Don't judge your child for what he sometimes does or doesn't do, he is in perfect balance. Learn to appreciate life with your child. Accept every situation, and if it looks bad to you, find the benefits. If it looks too good to be true, find the drawbacks. Always stay balanced and don't get attached to "good" times or be fearful of "bad" times. Appreciate life and all that it brings.

When it feels that you are always on the defensive with your child, look at the other side. When he is stubborn, admire his persistence in the situation. When he is argumentative and manipulative, admire his critical thinking skills. Looking at the other side of the coin will take the edge off.

One of Dr Demartini's favourite sayings is: "Regardless of what you have done or not done, you are worthy of love." This is very true for children with ADD/ADHD. They are criticised so often and sometimes feel "unworthy" that loving them makes a huge difference. Regular hugs, affirmations of love, notes in their lunch boxes or text books, an SMS or post on Facebook go a long way in assisting them to feel worthy. Love them for the special people that they are.

"It is estimated that those with ADD/ADHD receive 20 000 more negative messages by the age of 12 than those without the condition. They view themselves as fundamentally different and flawed. When a child with ADHD receives a drop or two of praise, it's like rain in the desert. He drinks it in and revels in it," says ADHD expert, Dr Ned Hallowell.

One of your greatest challenges as a parent of a child with ADD/ADHD will be dealing with all the opinions from family, friends, teachers and even complete strangers. Whatever you do or say, there will be people who support you and people who challenge you. Both opinions are there, in balance, as an expression of a loving universe that wants you to grow and evolve and express yourself to your maximum capacity. You need both to do this. So love and appreciate those who tell you you're wonderful and love and appreciate those who criticise and attack you – together they will help you to reach your goals.

SCHOOL

As a parent you will need to apply innovative ideas to help your child through school. Dreaded tables, fractions and reading... all of these can pose greater than normal challenges for a child with ADD/ADHD, if not handled in a proactive way. It helps to realise that all of us are ADD in certain areas of life. These areas may just not be very high on our value system. By linking these tasks to our "high-value" tasks, it makes them easier to achieve. The same goes for your child.

When my child arrived home and declared that he was unable to learn fractions at all, that it was too difficult and that he would never understand it, I had to think fast. Luckily for me, he went to horse riding lessons that afternoon. I enlisted the help of the horse riding teacher and asked her to do the whole lesson in fractions: Go one-third down the arena and turn ninety degrees right; then continue one-quarter of the way and turn ninety degrees left, and so on. He got off the horse at the end of the lesson and said: "Mommy, you need to explain fractions to me otherwise I cannot do horse riding anymore!" The problem was solved because he had become open to the idea of fractions and after that, he was like a sponge.

It also helps to break projects up into smaller projects, and assign a deadline for completing each step. Most of the time, we're given a deadline for when an entire school project needs to be completed. Start with the project the day your child receives it. Work on it every day and complete it at least a day or two before the deadline. The day before it is due, go for a milkshake (or a treat your child will specifically enjoy) and make sure he understands that this treat is because he completed his project before the deadline. When the next project arrives, remind him of the treat. This basic motivation will help him to start work immediately and to work at a steady pace, rather than leaving everything to the last minute.

This will have a huge impact on him as an adult with ADD/ADHD, as he will not procrastinate and know to be organised from a young age. This habit is specifically important with exams, as children with ADD/ADHD cannot always remember what they learned the day before, but somehow manage to remember last week in great detail. We always started with mind maps as soon as the first chapter in a specific subject was done. When he was younger, I would do the mind maps for him while he watched. I made them colourful with funny drawings and lots of rhymes. He helped with these and still remembers most of them to this day.

A month before the exams, we would study every Saturday, from 08:00 – 15:00. So by the time the exams rolled on, we were going through the work for the third time and it was clear what he remembered which mind maps had worked for him, and which hadn't. From that point, we could fine-tune them. By using this method, exams ceased to be stressful, because he was prepared and relaxed.

The subject of mind maps can take up a whole chapter on its own, but in short: Make them colourful and funny. Make sure they relate to things your child will understand.

In Economics, whenever the word "export" came up in a rhyme, Elna was the word we would use. For example; Elna is my friend who immigrated to Australia, so Elna = Export. Can't remember the planets in order? *My* (Mercury) *Very* (Venus) *Eager* (Earth) *Monkey* (Mars) *Jumps* (Jupiter) *Swiftly* (Saturn) *Under* (Uranus) *Nine* (Neptune) *Planets* (Pluto)

And again we come back to Dr Demartini's work: link the learning to their highest values and interests. I linked tables to karate, fractions to horse riding, his interest in the Pyramids to history, his enjoyment of our trip to Mauritius to Geography. You have to think way outside the box, until you can link hockey scores to maths and athletics to science.

When they had to learn the periodic table, we found a game on the internet and he loved playing it. Today he knows the periodic table perfectly and understands it. There are many, many games and computer programmes that can assist.

Determining your child's learning style will make life a lot easier. Does your child zoom in on the details, or step back for the broad view?

Determining how he learns, helps you to support his strengths and develop strategies that work for him.

I found that motivating my child with various incentives worked very well. We don't eat a lot of take-aways and he really enjoyed spending his own money; so, from the first year he wrote exams, we had a reward system. It looked something like this:

50% – 59%: R10 + ice cream
60% – 69%: R20 + milkshake
70% – 79%: R50 + hamburger
80% – 89%: R75 + pizza
90% – 99%: R100 + sushi
100%: R1 000 (he asked for this one to be added, and I would have been very glad to pay him this!)

As my son got older and the work got more difficult, the figures changed. I had to pay him R500 – R850 per exam, and make a huge fuss about how much pleasure it gave me to pay it to him, because he'd worked so hard. The biggest thrill for both of us came at the end of the exams, when he received his well-earned rewards!

Exams can be very stressful for kids with ADD/ADHD, especially if they start studying a month before the time. Rewarding them with an incentive that is important to them, takes the edge off.

For many of our kids, report cards only measure the things they're *not* doing well. So, make your own report card, where you measure skills that are important to you – like creativity or compassion. When your child comes home unhappy about his report card, you can pull out your own and show him all the times he showed leadership or good problem solving. You'll boost his self-esteem and allow him to see himself in a new light. Keep this up!

Justin Timberlake has ADD/ADHD. So does Richard Branson, Tatum Channing and Lisa Ling. In fact, the list of really accomplished people (and parents) with ADD/ADHD is very long. Share these facts with your child and challenge him to reach for the stars.

SLOW DOWN

You *must* take care of yourself. If you don't make yourself a priority – physically, emotionally and spiritually – you will become drained and exhausted, and have nothing left to give. If you feel like you're always giving, make an appointment for yourself once a week to do something you enjoy. Make sure you have "me" time. Life today is extremely taxing. Slow down and eliminate things, and make your life less complicated. For example, say no to non-critical homework sometimes. The teachers may be upset, but it'll save you stress – and frankly, is first grade homework really linked to success in later life?

Another way to slow down is to build and create traditions; Pancake Day or a weekly Technology-Free Tuesday. Traditions instil predictability and a simpler life, and kids with ADD/ADHD do much better in a solid, predictable environment.

It is important to stop trying to create the perfect world with everyone in it, perfectly happy. It's impossible. Stop trying to make everybody else happy, and focus a bit more on making yourself happy. Give your kids and your spouse a little bit more responsibility so that you can step up and say, "It's my job to be content with myself and to give you tools to succeed in life, but I am not responsible for your happiness." Your family will be stronger for it!

Take a proactive stance in helping teachers, friends, or spouses understand what you and your child struggle with, and how they can help. When you meet with your child's teacher, share his passions, interests and strengths. Include where he struggles, and add specific strategies that the teacher may apply to help him. You'll be giving the teacher an honest view of your child while giving her the tools to support him.

Do not allow your children to become victims. They are bright, creative, and full of energy. Don't let them use their ADHD as an excuse – instead, help them use their strengths and think strategically about their difficulties. Does he struggle to sit still through his homework? Brainstorm ways to make it easier; for example, sitting on an exercise ball while working. This helps with core muscle development which could be lacking.

Knowledge is your greatest weapon. Research ADHD and different practical strategies to handle it. Your child may struggle with focus and attention – it's part of who he is. However, you can educate yourself and find unique and creative tools for him to use in class. Are there alternative therapies that might work? If you arm yourself with knowledge, you will feel less overwhelmed, allowing you the mental and emotional freedom to be the best possible mom that you can be.

I found a "QEEG" to be invaluable. The QEEG gives a 3-D reconstruction of the brain activity, enabling you to see your unique pattern of mental strengths and weaknesses – areas of the brain where there is too little or too much activity, and areas that are not coordinating their activity the best they could. Once you can see the reason for the struggles on a brain level you can choose specifically where to train the brain to achieve your goals. It gave me a huge amount of information, and I could systematically work through each issue it pointed out. We solved "problems" my child was having, one at a time. He also started feeling better about himself, realising there was a specific reason that reading, or copying from the blackboard in class was stressful and difficult for him. As we did exercises to help correct his visual problems, his reading improved. He became more interested in doing the exercises and began to open up about what else he was having difficulty with. We became a team and that bond from working together still exists today, when technically, he should be a "difficult" teenager.

NORMALLY AN ADHD HOUSEHOLD IS SLEEP-DEPRIVED

Getting a good night's sleep can be a big problem for ADHD families. A British research study shows that three times as many children with ADHD have difficulty falling or staying asleep and 57 percent of the parents of ADHD children slept less than six hours a night. More than half of children get up four times during the night and almost half wake up before 6am. It doesn't take much to figure out what's going on here: when children are awake, it's hard for parents to get any sleep.

Sleep deprivation makes both adults and children irritable, impatient, and less efficient at everything they do. Adults who haven't had a good night's sleep are more likely to miss work. Studies show that not getting enough rest can make ADD/ADHD symptoms worse, leading to loss of emotional control. It can also adversely affect working memory, a problem many of our children suffer from.

There's a biological reason that children with ADHD tend to sleep less: Many of the same regions of the brain regulate both attention and sleep. So, a child who has attention problems is likely to have sleep problems too. You can't change your child's biology, but there are ADD/ADHD-friendly strategies to help children overcome their sleep problems. Here are some ideas:

Avoid sleeping pills

Most sleep medications that work well for adults haven't been adequately tested for safety and effectiveness in children.

Exercise is valuable

Have your child exercise (jog, jump rope, ride a bike, walk) in the morning or during the day. Physical activity helps our bodies make the transition between the phases of sleep. Since exercise places physical stress on the body, the brain increases the time a child spends in deep sleep.

Set a realistic bedtime and stick to it

Accept the fact that your child may need less sleep than other kids his age. If you put him to bed too early, there's a chance that he'll just lie there, wide awake, becoming increasingly anxious. Whatever bedtime you establish, enforce it consistently – on weekends as well as during the week. Letting your child stay up late on Friday and Saturday nights will disrupt his circadian clock; come Monday morning, he'll wake up with something similar to jet lag.

Night time rituals

Evening rituals signal the brain and body to slow down. The time in the hour leading up to your child's bedtime should be devoted to reading, listening to music, or a similar relaxing activity. Violent TV programmes and video games should be strictly off-limits at this time. Tell or read a bedtime story to a younger child. Allow older children to read in bed. Be sure your child has his favourite blanket or stuffed animal. Older kids may prefer to cuddle with a squishy, soft pillow.

Eating and drinking right before bedtime

Avoid eating and snacking from two to three hours before bedtime. Digestion, especially of foods containing caffeine or sugar, can keep your child up. Your child should drink enough water during the day to prevent asking for a glass of water at bedtime – and subsequent bathroom breaks later.

Keep the room dark

In addition to cueing your child for sleep time, darkness eliminates the visual distractions that keep him from falling asleep. If a child can't see his toys, he is less likely to get out of bed to play with them. If your child is afraid of the dark and needs a light on to fall asleep, make sure that the light is dim, and that it goes off once he falls asleep (use a timer).

Consider relaxation routines

Deep breathing or listening to soothing music can make it easier to fall asleep. A foot rub or back rub relaxes a restless child. Have your child focus on breathing while visualising an elevator gently ascending and descending with every inhalation and exhalation. Consider an evening prayer.

Sleep comfortably if dressed comfortably

- Chilly feet keep some children awake; wearing socks may send them into dreamland.
- Remove any scratchy tags from pyjamas.
- Don't combine flannel pyjamas and flannel sheets. The fabrics may stick together and make it difficult to turn over in bed.
- If the room is warm, all-cotton sleepwear can prevent sweating and tossing.
- Air conditioning or a fan will cool down the room – and the whirring sound of the fan blades can be calming.

Do it

Dealing with an ADD/ADHD child's sleep problem isn't easy, but it's worth the effort. Given the consequences of chronic sleep problems (for the entire family), it's best to take action sooner rather than later. Keep at it, it works.

Routines are very important and can make your child's (and your) life easier.

Create a routine for your child and keep a copy of it in a central location – like the kitchen or living room. For younger children, use pictures as well as text. You, your partner, caregivers and your child can reference it to make sure every day is consistent and everyone is following the schedule. If you laminate the routine, your child can use an erasable marker to cross out tasks he has completed.

Adding structure to your routine

- A written schedule is great, but don't stop there. Use other tools to make sure your family follows the routine every day.
- A kitchen timer helps your child stay on schedule.

- Calendars on smartphones allow you to set reminders.
- Behaviour charts can be used to reward your child for following the schedule.
- Keep the routine as simple as possible; elaborate routines often get tossed after a few weeks.

Your routine should be consistent, but that doesn't mean it isn't ever going to change. Your child's needs may change, an after-school activity might be added or be removed, your work schedule may change, or you may have miscalculated how long a task takes. If you realise the schedule isn't working, review the routine once a month, or sooner, and make adjustments to fit the facts.

THINGS YOU SHOULD NEVER SAY TO YOUR CHILD

People say insensitive things. ADD/ADHD myths and misinformation don't help. People blame us or our children for behaviours controlled by the condition, and we know it's wrong. But sometimes frustrating behaviours can push even the most loving parents to say things we quickly regret.

Parents aren't perfect – we all wish we could take back some of the harsh things we've said. But there are twelve phrases that parents of ADD/ADHD kids should absolutely, positively never say out loud:

1. "You're stupid. Are you really that stupid/lazy/crazy? Stop being so lazy! You know what you're doing! How many times do I have to show you?"
2. "I Love You, But..." Never, ever say"...*but*..."it should be "*I love you AND I can't let you...,*" or "*You made a bad choice AND I love you enough to...*"
3. "Why Can't You Be Normal? Why can't you be like the other kids?"
4. Don't ever say "What's wrong with you?"
5. Never, ever tell them, "You're not normal."
6. The social struggles faced by many children with ADHD stem from a feeling of being different and standing out, in a negative way, from

the other kids at school. Teach your child that his differences make him interesting and give him the social skills to make friends with other kids who will appreciate his strengths.

7. "If only you would apply yourself..."

8. "You're not even trying."

9. "You're so smart and talented! Why can't you just do the work?" The answer you'll get: *I don't know.*

   Focus is not a matter of willpower for kids and adults with ADD/ADHD. It is controlled by brain chemistry. The ADD/ADHD brain makes fewer neurotransmitters, like dopamine, which control focus and mood.

10. "Clearly, you didn't take your meds today."

11. "I wouldn't wish an ADD/ADHD child on anyone." Worse even: "I hope you have kids just like yourself" or "I wouldn't wish kids like you on anyone."

12. "You should be ashamed."

See your child for who and what he is: a uniquely created human being with special talents and ADD/ADHD in areas that are not high on his value system. I made the transformation, and faced the (very difficult but ultimately positive) decision to take my son out of school at the end of Grade 9. He is now studying water purification at college. He is up early and studies at least eight hours a day and is so far ahead in his studies, that he will write his first-year exams within 4 months. He is planning to write his second year 4 months later.

It may sometimes seem that you are not making any progress, or that you don't have any control. The demands of a child with ADD/ADHD can be extremely challenging and there will be some days where you are left feeling that you have completely failed. It helps to remember that consistency and routine will help you on days when you're tired or unable to be creative. Start every day new, and don't be too hard on yourself when things don't go perfectly. Success happens over a long time, with daily input. By reminding your child regularly that you love him and support him, and by creating a reliable framework for him to express himself in, you will be amazed at the things he will achieve!

Coming to terms with the challenges may be difficult at times but the transformation is really worthwhile!

Marisia Robus

Marisia started out in financial advertising and printing and became passionate about not having her child grow up with the label of ADHD and go through life like her husband did, feeling something is wrong with him and lacking confidence. She did a lot of research on ADHD and also tried a long list of alternative treatments, nothing was off limits to help her child.

She was introduced to the Demartini Method and found that it was a life saver and after she made the huge decision to take her child out of school and realised what a positive difference it made in his life, she did her training as a Demartini Method® Facilitator. She acquired more skills and approaches and is inspired to help parents and kids who have ADD/ADHD to realise their full potential..

While helping her friend and Wealth Psychologist and Master Demartini Method® facilitator, Ilze Alberts, sell her psychology practice of 14 years, she realised how helpless parents of kids with ADD/ADHD feel and how much knowledge she has amassed over the years. She started helping parents at the practice and this made her realise that she can help parents by sharing her mistakes and successes.

"If I can help one child have a more fulfilled life by what I have learned and help the parents feel good about themselves as parents and stop blaming themselves, then I have achieved my goal" she says.

She is passionate about sharing all her practical experience and lessons learned over 17 years with other parents who feel as if they are fighting a losing battle.

Contacts:
www.marisiarobus.com
info@marisiarobus.com

Life Happens

Three years ago, If you had asked me to define "Awareness to Transformation", I would've given a layman's explanation and this would've been my response:

Awareness: Knowing the problem.

Transformation: Changing in line with the knowledge gained from knowing the problem.

Today I would give you another definition, still layman but more in depth based on my experiences of the past few years.

This is the story of so many people affected by HIV and AIDS. It's not *my* story, it's not *your* story, it is OUR story!

We were sitting on a couch in her home and she was very upset about what she had just been asked to do. She couldn't see herself raising another child. What did he think of her? How could he ask her to do this? Why did he ask her to do this? This child was from a woman of a different race, how would she cope with cultural differences and people traipsing in and out of her home?

I remember giving her all the reasons why she had to do this, how it was the right thing to do, how the child was family and couldn't be ignored. How, if she didn't take him, she would never stop worrying; wondering where he was, what he was doing, if he was eating, did he have clothes, was he warm, was he okay, what he looks like and so on and so forth: how cultural differences would not be an obstacle as he would only know the culture into which he was raised, how you made the rules to prevent people traipsing in and out of your home. You know what I'm talking about.

She was a wonderful, warm, kind woman, whose home was always filled with laughter and joy. Her heart and home were opened to many people. Her personality endeared her to others. She was a good listener and people found it easy to talk to her. She was wise, really cared and loved being surrounded by lots of people. She worried when the homeless didn't come to ask her for something to eat. The aromatic scents of sweet and savoury lingered in her home because there was always something cooking or baking in her kitchen. She was old school and loved feeding her guests.

She taught me to push myself and strive for more; for better. She got me my first job. She loved music and instilled that love in me. She sang and danced in her home. She created a homely home for her children and deprived them of nothing! She worked hard to ensure that they had the best that she could give them. She gave even when she didn't have much and when she didn't have much, she gave of herself. It was amazing to be around her. At gatherings, wherever there was the most laughter was where you would find her. There is no hagiography here, I knew the good and I knew the bad!

She took the child in and loved and nurtured him. She took such good care of him that her own Daughter developed an angry jealousy towards him. A jealousy that was well hidden. The thing with jealousy is that it is not something that finds satisfaction in hiding. It finds a way out through the things that we say and the things that we do when we think that no-one is paying attention. It rears its head through body language; the longer it is hidden, the more careless becomes the carrier.

We heard that his mother was sick and in and out of hospital on an ongoing basis. Our suspicions were confirmed when we were told that she had died of AIDS and we were scared! Scared for the child, afraid of the child! It was an awful time.

The child's father immigrated with promises that he would support the child. He married, his wife didn't want any part of a child who had AIDS and gave him an ultimatum. He stopped supporting the child and left her with unexpected responsibilities. She had retired a few years earlier and her own had squandered the money that she had spent so many years building up for her retirement. Her husband had divorced her, her sons were in another country, living their own lives, her daughter was out of control, pleading poverty and making demands! She found herself without an income.

She baked and cooked and sold the food to keep the household afloat. She swallowed her pride and when there was no other way, borrowed money to keep them going. She pleaded with her own to provide for her, as they had promised to do when she found out that they had robbed her of all her finances. She pleaded with him to take care of his son. She only asked for what she needed; what she didn't have because they had behaved so shamelessly and spent her pension fund on who knows what!

They always had excuses, disguised as good reasons, for why they were unable to follow through on their commitments to her. Through all of this she continued to hope and pray and would not speak a bad word against them but we knew. We knew how they had neglected her, we knew how the daughter that she had prayed and longed for, was doing things that she could and would not tell us about. We knew that she was struggling. Her sister from another town would help where she could. I was caught up in my own life, more often unemployed than not. Things were bad, though none of us really knew just how bad.

She became more and more despondent, sank into a black pit of depression, became nasty and vicious and turned into someone who I didn't know. She had lost her glow; her sparkle. It was as though the reality of her situation had beaten all the good right out of her. I spoke to her about this once. I told her that I missed her. I told her how I needed to hear her childlike innocent, bubbly laughter. I spoke openly about her vicious tongue that cut through people like a sharp, serrated blade. I spoke about how bitter she had become. I spoke from the heart and said many things that everyone had wanted to say and didn't. I loved her and I know that she knew the place that I was coming from. She promised to try, she said that she hadn't realised that it was that bad and that she would try to be better. My heart broke for her. I know that she believed that she tried even though she didn't really believe that things were as bad as I was saying.

People were pulling away from her, they were not visiting as much and they would avoid engaging in conversation with her. It was just her, the daughter, the child and misery.

I will never forget how much she wanted a daughter. She longed for a little girl that she could dress up in girly clothes, a child whose hair she could braid and to whom she could pass on so many things. During her pregnancy she told me that I had to buy earrings for the child. She was convinced that she was carrying a girl. When I asked her what she would do with the earrings if it was another boy, she just laughed and said that she would pierce his ears and that he would wear the earrings. Her heart was filled with joy when she gave birth to her precious little girl. Everyone around her felt her elation. She had the same song in her heart when she gave birth to each of her children but for her this was a dream come true. She doted on her daughter, the brothers always looked out for their little sister and were protective of her and life was good, everything was right with her world.

But things change. Our experiences can break our spirit and turn us into something we would never have imagined that we could become.

She became ill very slowly. She got progressively worse and eventually died. This meant that the child was left in the care of a jealous daughter with a child of her own, that she didn't really want to take care of either. The child had a Father who didn't care, Uncles who didn't want to know, Cousins who were concerned and Grand Aunts who were worried about him but were to afraid to expose their own grand children to a child with AIDS. Everyone cared, everyone was concerned, everyone said what a lovely child he was, everyone was afraid to expose themselves, their children and or their grandchildren to him by providing him with a loving and stable home.

The child lived with the daughter for a while until she couldn't manage anymore. She had financial constraints, emotional constraints, had just lost her mother, was separated from her husband, had her own child to take care of, and, and, and.

The daughter moved him to a small town, to live with a relative in a big, lonely house located on huge grounds. I can empathise and I acknowledge that it could not have been easy for any young woman. She totally isolated herself from all family and only kept in contact with her brothers. We heard unpleasant things about her behaviour, things that I did not confirm because she and I were as estranged at that time, as we are now. Perhaps she cut all ties because she wanted to live the type of life that she had chosen for herself. Who knows, maybe she was ashamed of how she had received the things that she felt she deserved. I don't know, she never spoke and neither did I.

The social media family group was abuzz with conversations about what was happening to the child.

The Aunts and Cousins were at their wits end because the Father was not willing to live up to his responsibility and refused to acknowledge or provide for the child. There had been many hard conversations with a lot of disrespect and hurtful things said. Aunts were sworn and called some colourful names and still the child was not settled.

So, yes we were educating ourselves on AIDS and how it was transmitted and still, this situation was too close for comfort. We understood more about this disease than we did before it came into our lives and still we were worried about how we would manage the disease and keep those uninfected children, uninfected.

He was moved from pillar to post, didn't go to school, got more and more sick and eventually developed epilepsy and wet himself with each episode.

The daughter found his sister, who took him in because she said she loved him and would take care of him. Something take care of him. This suited the daughter and the Uncles because he was far removed from the family and maybe they thought he happened and she sent him to the other sister who took him in because she said she loved him and would disappear. The other sister lived in a neighbouring country. Then something happened and she asked that the child be returned to the Daughter.

I heard talk that the Daughter had become a woman of ill repute and that she had asked her siblings to adopt her own child as she could not take care of him. I cannot confirm this and hope that it is not true.

Through all the ooh-ing and aah-ing, the angry words, the suggestions, the pleas and the possible solutions, the child remained displaced. Eventually there was a solution, the child would live with his Father's family. A woman who lived alone, in a big house and who was known to have taken care of children previously. The child would travel back to his country of birth and move in with this woman who had so much love to give. It was agreed, or so we thought!

The Uncles decided that it would cost too much to have him travel with a woman who travelled between the countries on business; a woman well known by two of the Aunts. The Uncles took a decision to stop all arrangements and said that they would make the required travel arrangements to have the child transported back to his country of birth. We all waited with bated breath for the move to happen so that the child could be settled. Again, things fell through and the child was not settled. The Uncles had once again failed to deliver on their promises. We were all very angry and eventually decided to take things into our own hands and make whatever arrangements were necessary to place the child into a loving home. We were disgusted by the behaviour displayed by the Uncles and the petty quibbling over money when they and/or their families were travelling all over the world. They were openly discussing their travels and travel plans, with no regard for the child or his stabilisation.

Out of courtesy and a desire to do things right, the Father was again consulted. We were told that the Father agreed and the arrangements were made.

Those involved in the repatriation of this child did not exhale until the child was comfortably settled. He is receiving the love, care and attention that he deserves. He is receiving the medical care that is his right. He is receiving the counselling that should have happened a long time ago. He is finally settled and I pray that we did and that we continue to do all that we can for this boy.

I often think about how different things would have been for him if She had lived. I wonder what She would say about how things have unfolded.

I think about the child and how he could be feeling. How confused he must be, how neglected he felt. I only hope that one day, he will know that he was never far from our thoughts or our hearts. That we did what we could and that we tried to create the stability that She would've wanted for him.

Mostly, I think about the time when he is going to ask questions that we are going to find so difficult to answer. Questions like: Why didn't my Dad want me? Why am I not living with my Mother's family? Why was I sent away? Why were the promises made, not kept? Why, why, why, why, why?

I can't think of how we can prepare for these questions but I do know that we don't have much time before they come. It is a time that I am not looking forward to facing but it is a time that will change and affect many, many people, in so many different ways.

Don't judge!

How has my definition changed from a few years ago?

Awareness: Knowing the problems that we are facing.

Transformation: A conscious decision to understand the knowledge gained through awareness and to set in motion a set of behaviours that will move one from where we are, to the best possible solution, for that particular time.

I would add a footnote saying: "Not everyone will be pleased with the outcome achieved"

Shereen Elmie

I was born in Cape Town in the colourful District Six, on the 27 April 1961. My Dad took up a position in the then Rhodesia, where I completed my schooling. In 1980, much to the dismay of my parents, I moved back to South Africa and settled in Johannesburg. My parent's big fear was that I was returning to an apartheid South Africa, where anyone who was not white, did not have any real rights. As they recounted the stories of their experiences, I became aware that their main reason for leaving South Africa was to provide a better life for their children. It was unfortunate that I was reminded that we had been living in a Rhodesia that had very much the same laws, albeit unnamed. The only reason why we were allowed to use the Public Toilets in the City Centre was because my Aunt was "in charge".

My return to South Africa had been uneventful, except for one incident when I was blissfully unaware of the discomfort of the other patrons, when my "then" husband joined me for my morning coffee. We were refused service in a tiny coffee shop that I had been frequenting for about eighteen months. The owner apologised profusely, explaining that he thought I was Portuguese! Although we were angry and embarrassed at the time, we were soon laughing about it!

I run a Learning and Development company called Step It Up Training. Our most recent project is delivering community based work readiness programmes to Grades 11 and 12's, to afford them every opportunity, when they enter the job market.

Website: www.stepituptraining.co.za
Email: shereen@stepituptraining.co.za
sherelmie@gmail.com
Tel: 0799817208/0766024803

The Opportunity in
the Rock Bottom

The penny dropped when my fiancé left. Unlike my normal verbal self, it was impossible for me to make any comment when I had no heart left from which to speak. The tightness in my chest made me gasp for air. I wasn't even sure where the strength for my next breath would come from. The emptiness in my belly left me full with worthlessness. My head pounded and all I could hear was pain. Nausea trickled through my body, thick like concrete, eventually setting in my chest. And the sensations continued long after he left.

I felt alone and judged. I felt frustrated and angry. I felt inadequate and disappointed, too.

Alone and judged because I am, in fact all of us are, a work in progress. I couldn't have been more committed to self-improvement, self-betterment and self-actualization. It was *because* of my imperfections that I strived endlessly to be the best person I could be. I didn't just talk the talk; every day of my life I was pushing myself to learn, to improve, to be a better person. And now, the person I loved most in the world was telling me that all this wasn't enough.

Frustrated and angry because I knew without doubt that I would never do anything that was outright disrespectful and hurtful to my fiancé. And yet here he was suggesting in no uncertain terms that I had done exactly that. I admitted that in the past I had struggled to understand respect and boundaries – others' and mine – but those were my lessons to learn; I was on the learning curve. I was seething at how hideously my behaviour had been interpreted. The injustice made me pitiful.

Inadequate and worthless because he questioned whether *I* was the marrying kind. "There are things about you that I need to wrap my brain around," he said. "It's not my commitment I question but yours." And then he asked, "Are you being honest with yourself?" For the first time a man was about to rip away my happiness. And apparently it was *my* behaviour (which I had justified as harmless to anyone who would listen) that had given him cause to doubt my feelings for him.

The truth is, I had an addiction – an emotional addiction. I craved men's approval and validation. My ego couldn't get enough of it. Holding glances longer than I needed along with other 'innocent' interactions were my lifeblood. Being light and full of laughter, flirting with intelligence, charming men with compliments and carefully considered words of endearment were intoxicating for me. Provocative and sexual movements, coffee dates and mixed messages, saying one thing and meaning another. I was well versed and practiced at all these strategies. Before long there was a string of men lining up to get to know me better, vying for my attention, hoping for more. And *this* became my sustenance.

I didn't need their physical touch; it was merely their admiration I coveted. In fact, I sought just enough praise to fill the void my father had created. He had been a dad who provided well financially for his daughters but who gave little emotionally. No blame exists, but this primary male relationship – the one on which future relationships would be founded – left me feeling unloved. My devotees stepped in. Where my father had failed, their attention succeeded in drowning out any possible thoughts that I might be unlovable.

It wasn't a coincidence that I had made a career for myself in the perfect industry to feed my addiction. Fans and followers are easy to come by when you work as an international model. With the added lure of this label, it was easy to coax a man into a fantasy with me. I cringe at how self-absorbed and egocentric I was back then. The fact that sex wasn't part of the arrangement simply masked the ugly, self-serving behaviour to which I had become addicted. I wanted their validation. I hungered to hear their words of adulation. I pieced all their proclamations together until I felt truly desirable, totally lovable. And that was all I wanted to feel.

It took that fateful day, when the man of my dreams opened my eyes, to see my ugliness. He did it without naming, blaming or shaming me. He simply left. "I love you," he said, "but I cannot live with someone who needs men stroking her ego to feel good about herself. I'm not asking you to change – you are who you are. But I can't live with that person anymore." He then closed the door gently behind him.

At first I denied that it was me who had a problem. My behaviour was not *that* bad. Was it? I never slept with any of them. I wasn't caught having sex behind his back. Surely a bit of flirting was harmless. Wasn't it? I was committed to my fiancé. It was simply that I enjoyed the playful attention of more than one man. How could he use this to destroy what *we* had?

Then a friend spelled it out for me. "But Shelley," she said, "that's just who you are. You've always been like that. One man will never be enough for you."

Perhaps my fiancé was right; maybe I was not the marrying kind. Never before had I been willing to give up my ways, even when they caused endless troubles in my relationships. My behaviour was innocent, I believed. I was right in my innocence. So what if I was a master of deceit? A wizard at sending mixed messages? I reeled men in and out as proficiently as a fly-fisherman. I didn't care about them. I only cared about me. And that was where the truth lay. *I only cared about me.* In the heady moments spent in the company of other men, I had ignored how my behaviour made my partner feel. Isn't that what addiction is? A single-minded yearning to satisfy one's own needs, with no consideration for the effect on others?

The irony of it all. A teetotaler, who gets drunk on the whiff of a glass of wine, with a dependency as controlling as a Class A drug. It didn't bother me; I wasn't the one suffering. Only my partner suffered. But then the day came when he decided 'No thanks. Not for me' and I realized that this was going to be the constant and miserable story of my life. How could I want this for my future? How could this possibly ever make me happy? At first I did what addicts do: I looked for someone to blame. My Dad's lack of emotional presence in my childhood came sharply into focus. But the truth was I needed to look even closer to home and I needed to do it fast, because I was busy destroying the most treasured part of my life. The one person I could not bear to lose had just walked out on our pending engagement and me.

It's called Rock Bottom. It's when you can't bear to look in the mirror and see the reflection of someone you despise. Looking back at me I saw someone unworthy, a person crammed with guilt, shame, humiliation and other self-hating and destructive emotions. It might not have been my partner's conscious choice to deliver me a heavy dose of tough love, but his walking out on me undoubtedly forced my rock bottom. Nights of loneliness. Not wanting to be with anyone other than him. Wondering who he might be with. The tables had turned.

But it was this that inspired realness. For the first time I began an honest conversation with myself. It would become the pivotal point for my vulnerability, hope, self-forgiveness and self-compassion. Where previously I had filled my mind with delusions of denial and illusions of my innocence, from the barren and burnt landscape of loss, sincerity emerged. Like fynbos shoots bursting through scorched earth, accountability and authenticity grew. I wanted to be a better person – someone who I could be proud to be, who my fiancé would be proud to be married to and who my friends would be proud to know. I wanted to be deserving of the connected and meaningful relationship I now desired more than anything. I became aware of my own shallowness, the trivial way with which I had treated other people. Most of all, I realized that my fiancé had been justified in believing that I would let him down, humiliate him and jeopardize the sanctity of our marriage. I didn't want to be that person. I wanted more for myself and for him. I wanted my life to illustrate integrity, loyalty and kindness. But from where I was standing, I couldn't have been further away from those things.

At times I wondered if I would ever be happy again. Then, I found my coach and my recovery journey began. I was determined to be that particular leopard who could indeed change its spots. Coaching taught me to take responsibility for the state of my life. My coach helped me believe that I could create any life that I wanted, as long as I knew what it was I wanted. It *could* be done. If my life was the result of the choices I'd made, then I could start making new choices. I knew that the time had come when I needed to be painfully honest with myself. I had to discover who I was and who I wanted to become, and be okay with the chasm between the two. I became conscious of the times when I was aligned with the person I wanted to be and recognized those when I was way off. When I relapsed into old habits, I took ownership of my behaviour, without judgment, and noted the precursors that triggered this regression. I became practiced at identifying the conditions that aggravated or supported my 'weakness' so that I could learn to avoid them at all costs. It was an arduous, painful and exposing process, but before long there were glimmers of the person I wanted to be – one I liked, one I trusted. Best of all, I started to attract back into my life the respect of the one man I loved.

Not many men would have put up with the pain I put him through in our early days. He was, and still is, a gift to me. Once he knew I was serious about my 'recovery', he supported me and watched as the men whittled down in numbers until they were reduced to only him. And then he agreed to be my husband. I have become the woman I was hoping to be and the wife I knew he deserved. Thirteen years on and ten wedding anniversaries later, I am proud to call myself a devoted and loyal wife.

With marriage I decided it was time to change careers. Having experienced first hand the power of coaching, I decided this was where my passion now lay. In a short period of time I had shifted what traditional therapy had not done for me in years. It had given me a shift in perspective. A new life. A new me. And now I wanted to be able to help others.

Transformation is a process not an event. It takes consciousness and awareness with every step of the journey. Many times we might slip back into our old ways, but then we have the benefit of learning from *that* experience as well. We discover and avoid the trigger situations, environments or people where we know we are most likely to trip up. With practice we create spaces between 'me, my thoughts and my actions'. We learn that 'I am not my thoughts and actions, I am the observer behind them'. We become mindful of who is showing up in any moment. We start to distinguish the 'old me' from the 'work in progress me' from the 'mindful me'. I like to think of relapse as a part of failing forward – just another part of the process. And it's the only way to learn, to grow and evolve. Some bad habits we can eradicate by going cold turkey, but with others (like eating, sex and love addictions) it is a dedicated process of weaning yourself off the bad stuff, one day at a time. Each day is a new day to redefine who you want to be. Each day we are given the opportunity to live life more deliberately than the day before.

Coaching is at its essence a methodology for change. The currency of a coach is the questions they ask. It is a collaborative partnering, which requires reflection and introspection. The process demands we get clear about a few things. What is the change you seek? What is the future you would rather have? Where are you now with regards to that future and what are the small steps or giant leaps you can take towards it? What are the obstacles in your way? What is the cost of change? It is always easier to stay the same unless you are willing to endure the discomfort and inconvenience married to change. What are you willing to suffer for? What capabilities do you need to nurture? Who do you need to become to do what you need to do in order to have what you really want? How will that make a difference in your life? And why is that so compelling for you?

Recently, I attended a workshop on addiction. "You've got to force rock bottom." This was the professional (and personal) advice from an ex-addict running a recovery and rehab programme on how *not* to enable your loved ones to continue along a path of self-destruction. Tough Love is the only way to go, apparently. It is harsh and painful for both the addict and friends and family. But from my own experience, I have to agree. Unconditional love would not have helped me. It is not about finding someone who loves us unconditionally; it is about being with someone who can open our eyes so that we love *ourselves* unconditionally. Love is unconditional but relationships are not. Healthy relationships and functional, self-loving people have boundaries. They do not accommodate any and all behaviour unconditionally. This I had learnt firsthand.

When we love ourselves we don't allow people to hurt us. By exposing ourselves to those who hurt us, we fail to show ourselves any kindness or tenderness. We are not loving and gentle toward ourselves when we allow someone to abuse us. Boundary setting is the first step to loving oneself. Saying "No, I will not tolerate the intolerable" can be the greatest act of love we can show another and ourselves. By not allowing someone to engage in hurtful/destructive/disrespectful behaviour, you are teaching them how both of you deserve to be treated. It took my fiancé's unfaltering demonstration of self-love to open my eyes.

Listening to the keynote speaker discuss addiction, I felt myself tingle with the resonance of her words. I too am an ex-addict who takes people through recovery and rehabilitation. But in my line of work, it is self worth that we rehabilitate. I have been 'clean' for over a decade. I created new friendships with people who were not vested in me staying the same. I avoided the people, places and environments that kept me stuck, until my empowering inner voice was louder than the destructive voice. My re-invention not only saved my relationship, it left me passionate about helping others change and transform themselves.

I have been a qualified coach for eight years. Both my personal and professional experience shows me, without a shred of doubt, that through awareness followed by transformation, we can create meaningful lives with deeply connected relationships. There is a saying in the helping profession, 'You cannot take someone where you have never been yourself'. Because my career was born from my wounds, I feel equipped to help others successfully navigate their own relationships – both with themselves and significant others. I am *still* a work in progress. But it was the combination of rock bottom and coaching that gave me the mental rinse I needed. I had been operating on old, outdated programs that didn't serve me anymore. Fortunately, I can rely on certain friends, colleagues and family members to point out when I veer off my path of recovery. Overall, however, I now quite like who I am. Fifteen years after I hit rock bottom, and despite being less toned more squidgy, less smooth more wrinkly, less thin more voluptuous – you get the idea – *now* I love being in my skin.

Some people seem to live quite contently in their skin. They feel at peace with who they are, know what they want and need for their sense of wellbeing, and have the courage to pursue those things as well as *believing they deserve all the good stuff.* For many of us it is a long, hard slog. It took me half a lifetime to figure it out. And the conclusion I came to is this:

When the *why* is big enough, the *how* is not an issue. Surrender to the pain. Forgive yourself. Be compassionate of your faults. Believe in your magnificence. When you feel like you have sold your soul because you have sacrificed your honour and integrity, you haven't. In the words of C.S. Lewis: 'We don't have a soul, we are a soul.' We cannot sell our souls; we can merely betray the essence of who we are. Until we don't. People make choices and their choices make them. Making a new choice to preserve our integrity, to respect those around us and indeed ourselves, happens in each moment. When we have the courage to take stock of our lives and have an honest relationship with ourselves, our spiritual development blossoms.

Get honest. Get open. Get vulnerable. We can alter ourselves any day, at any time in our lives. And so it will be, from rock bottom, with awareness and through transformation you will reveal the true essence of yourself.

Shelley Lewin

Shelley Lewin is an ICF accredited 'Solution Focused Brief Coach' and SACAP Counsellor and Coach who divides her time between performance/leadership coaching in the corporate arena and life/relationship coaching in her private practice. She is dedicated to the understanding and development of intra-personal and interpersonal relationships and has been facilitating transformation from her private practice since 2007. Known by the readers of her blog and listeners of her local radio slot as *'The Relationship Architect'*,

Shelley brings a wealth of knowledge and experience (personal and professional) in individual and couple development. Her website www. TRAcoaching.com presents the scope of her coaching and facilitation work as well houses Shelley's informative blog.

Prior to her career in Counselling and Coaching, Shelley worked in the Fashion and Beauty Industry for 15 years working and living in 20 countries; calling four different continents home. Having travelled extensively and been exposed to a myriad of cultures, Shelley has come to learn that regardless of age, race, faith, location and culture, we all share the same fundamental needs as human beings and that the state of our lives can be attributed to feelings of worthiness. Every human being wants to be validated, to be heard, to feel that what they have to say matters. Because we are 100% responsible for our lives, we have the ability to choose how we respond to circumstances and the choices we make for ourselves. This is where her clients' successes exist i.e. the increasing ability to be mindful of all the options available and then to consciously make choices that serve them and their relationships.

The Call to Awaken
- My story of living in Awareness and Transformation

Chapter Contributed by Diane Collier

Every fork in the road offers two paths from which to choose: the one you "should" take and the one which calls from within most often as just a whisper. Some say it's the heart, others the soul. Either way it's the call to adventure to life and living.

Receiving the Invitation to participate in this collective effort was surprising and inspiring as it re-awakened the seed of something which had arisen after attending a breakfast event towards the end of 2014. The idea was to create a forum for personal stories, specifically amongst women and where this shared wisdom could be of comfort and guidance to others facing their cross-roads. Excitement sparked as I read the requirements for the inaugural edition, which included this written contribution and those feelings were was soon followed by some creative angst. Here I was facing my fork in the road.

I love writing even though it comes with a lot of creative angst. It's a funny thing professing to love something yet being equally uncomfortable. This reminds me of when I began facilitating workshops a few years back which had me feeling alive, on purpose, joyous and totally terrified all at once. In the end I'm happy to say the love of facilitating prevailed.

What is this push-pull and does it have anything to do with awareness and transformation? It seems to be related to producing the *Big Ask* of oneself where ironically fear and the highest personal reward share the same space in our inner world the life lesson of balancing what we desire with our concerns of it coming true. Moving out the comfort zone is the only way we stretch ourselves and some times we do so genuinely curious and other times we resist all the way. I'm sure this situation is familiar to many of you.

It turns out the actual experience of creating this contributory chapter is the ideal subject matter, as it contains all the elements of the journey from awareness to transformation. My personal challenge has been to transcend the concerns of an expected outcome and external validation and to trust the process of creation. In doing so, my sincere hope is that this leap of faith will be a source of inspiration to nudge or perhaps greatly inspire you to take action in the direction of your most authentic desires.

The Journey of Change in a nutshell

Thought starts as energy and arrives in our awareness from out of the sea of pure potentiality. Words are our attempt to embody thought and feeling and connect us into personal meaning which makes our mental maps and experience more 'real'. Right now, I'm aware of 'transcribing' seeds of possibility into words, so as to connect with you and convey a shared spark of understanding.

Our ability to recognise and make sense of a given concept is guided by how much it matches our conditioned reality. The same is true of feedback in that it needs to make enough sense so we can acknowledge and learn from the experience. When we wholeheartedly respond to the new awareness received from feedback it becomes wisdom. Some refer to this process as the ability to empty our cup of knowing so as to allow new knowledge received to become wisdom within.

The journey of change requires us to continually go beyond the conditioned mind and its reality into deeper unknown areas to bring about new awareness. It requires being open to consider what else is possible that we have not allowed for. By the time we find ourselves noticing what we have not previously noticed, our inner world has already shifted and how we experience reality is influenced by this new awareness.

I wonder what you do *not know* about yourself, that if you were to, would change everything?

Awareness

Awareness requires energy and space. It's the allowance for something new to emerge. You know that feeling when you realise you have become a different person. When everything is the same yet different. What you don't know is when and how it happened. Eckhart Tolle refers to awareness as the "space in which thoughts exist when that space has become conscious of itself". We can deepen this awareness by staying out of conclusion. Start by asking yourself questions like 'what else is possible here' and 'what's right about this I'm not getting'. Both are great questions for creating more space for inner knowing and greater awareness to emerge.

There's a wonderful Ted Talk by Elisabeth Gilbert http://www.ted.com/talks/elizabeth_gilbert_on_genius?language=en#t-13006

about managing the emotional risk of creating, where in ancient Greece and Rome it was believed that creativity came from another mysterious external source. The Greeks referred to this as Damons, the Romans called it Genius. These disembodied creative companions would assist the human being and got all the credit for good work and the blame if it was a disappointment.

Times changed and the understanding came about that creativity flows from within us and this new perception brought all sorts of emotional turmoil for the Creatives with regard to their work being accepted or rejected. I feel the same by writing this, yet what I do know is that this invitation could not go unheeded. You know that feeling when your soul recognises transformation? In days gone by I would have deliberated far longer. This time it was easy to say Yes! and trust this *yes*. How much are you willing to be a contribution to stimulating your and others awareness? This is the kind of question we need to keep reminding ourselves of. The very act of responding has provided so much more awareness due to the gift of this very experience and I know it will continue to open even deeper awareness.

What about Transformation?

The journey of transformation results in higher consciousness because it involves overcoming inner fear. The old crumbles away and the emergence is of something new, more aware and more evolved.

In my own life and ever since I can remember I have enjoyed words, especially those which allow the imagination to explore being drawn deeper and deeper into the mystery of an unfolding story. The one who all the credit goes to for igniting this spark is Lulu, my grandfather from my mother's side. We adored his mischievous antics as he somehow managed to pull a never ending stream of stories and jokes right out the proverbial hat, delighting and entertaining grandchildren and adults alike. Wherever he was you would find us shrieking in laughter and delight.

During my second year of school around age 7, our class teacher introduced a daily ritual which had me spellbound and falling in love with stories. Every afternoon for about 10 minutes before going home, she would read *The Hobbit* and I would leave mesmerized dreaming of being in Hobbit-Land and almost unable to contain my excitement for the next days saga. The story of The Hobbit is an adventurous journey of transformation and I was totally hooked.

As a growing child I was also a real chatterbox and would drive my mother 'mad' so she says with never ending questions and conversation. Like my grandfather I could tell stories and they were mostly of magical creatures who had special powers. There was no difference between my imagination and the real world and those stories literally fell off my tongue.

However life lessons present themselves to all of us in interesting ways and one day was with a friend in our play-play world and got severely reprimanded by a family member for not telling the *truth*. I was mortified and totally humiliated. Other similar reprimands finally had me loosing interest in carefree magical stories and by the time I was 12 had become quite self-conscious and introverted in nature. Instead of interacting with others I had begun to favour the inner peace found in books and daydreams.

I believe my choice of study after school was subconsciously influenced by wanting to better understand myself and others. This took me in the direction of exploring psychology, sociology and specifically the dynamics of interpersonal relationships. What was not realised at the time is that for most of my adult life, I had felt a low level depression and ended up in the field of personal development where I found much relief with NLP, coaching, HeartMath and yoga. I was also drawn to more spiritual teachings which explored the world of personal mastery. All of this was my way of healing 30 plus years of being in judgment of the wrongness of myself and others. Along the way, whilst 'figuring out life', I have met some incredible healers, teachers and companions. Somewhere in all this my own transformation became apparent as a new awareness emerged which I noticed as greater inner well being, confidence and happiness.

Even though I shut down telling stories as a child, the stories never left me. They are in every place I have travelled to and right here where I live surrounded by shelves brimming with books on mindfulness, philosophy, self help, business, psychology, sociology, spirituality, love, life, animals, travel, health, yoga, cycling and well being. All things that lead to the expansion of one's soul and each one chosen with so much love and care as they represent the childhood dreams of hope and discovering something new ... and then there are all the spontaneous Aha moments of new Awareness which add to the uniqueness of our personal story!!

It turns out I have a great love for communicating and this has been allowed to blossom as I have come to realise the gift words can provide for transformation. The past 15 years have been very fortunate as I found my own footing step by step supported by great teachers and mentors. Every one of them has had the gift of facilitating the transformation of others. They certainly believed in me and now it is my turn to assist others in their transformation. At the end of the day, we all need to walk our own authentic path and if we can do so with a couple of spirited others, it makes the journey all that more interesting and enjoyable.

There's a wonderful story told by one of my teachers about humanity's deepest truth, which involves Cupid the God of Love. One day Cupid is reclining idly on his throne, watching the commotion around him. The Earth had finally been finished and Human kind was about to be set free upon the planet. But the Greek Gods had one final problem to solve before setting their creation in motion.

The problem was, where to hide the ultimate truth. Where would they hide their power from humanity? Cupid, God of Love, was getting bored of the discussion, but he sat through it, grudgingly listening to his elders.

Zeus, the God of the Heavens and all things, rumbled: *"Why not hide it in the furthest reaches of outer space? Man would never think to search there."* The other Greek Gods and Goddesses thought about it. But, eventually, Cupid pointed out that man would learn how to build some sort of craft that would be able to fly to the furthest reaches of the galaxies and find all the answers.

So the Olympians thought for a while. Then Poseidon, the God of the Seas, said: *"Why not hide it at the bottom of the ocean, in the deepest darkest place under the sea?"* Again after much talking Cupid, God of Love, said that man would eventually be able to adventure into and navigate the depths and find this treasure.

So again there was silence, until Demeter, the Goddess of the Earth, said: *"Why not hide it within the earth? In the center of the Earth, in its very heart."* Again the response came from Eros that humanity would find its way even down near the molten heart of the earth.

Hephaestus, the Fire God, eventually said: *"Well what of fire? Surely they'll never be able to find it there?"* But again came the response that some how man would find a way to distil fire and find the essence of all things.

It was then that Cupid the God of Love said, *"What of human kind itself. Why not hide it in the very last place they would look".* All the other Gods asked the little God where that would be?

"Why," Cupid said: *"In their hearts, inside themselves. They would never think to look there."*

A question to ponder from this tale is how does it relate to you? How much of your time is spent looking outside yourself for answers? How much do you listen to your heart and your own answers? In this asking of yourself, you begin to know thyself and develop the consciousness for more in your life to be made possible.

My invitation to you is to reflect on how many transformations you have been through. *What have you become by the experiences? Where is the gift in that for you and others?*

Everything you want is on the other side of fear

The main theme of this book is to facilitate greater awareness and I truly hope we do this for you. As mentioned, writing this chapter started off with a mix of excitement and creative jitters which quickly dissipated into the rewarding feeling that this potentially could make a difference to others on their journey from awareness to transformation.

The new awareness I have from this very experience is a sense of deeper connection to humanity and on a soul level there is much peace.

What Invitation can you Be to invite others to their greatness?

Commit to something that takes you beyond your comfort zone and self image. Something which allows your light to shine and gives permission for others to do the same (thank you Marianne Williamson for these powerful words). This is where you being you, truly are the gift you be to this world and to yourself.

I feel such immense joy in writing this contributory chapter. How much did awareness, transformation and choice have to do with this?

Probably everything ☺

Diane holds a B Soc Sci degree, is an ACC Certified Executive Coach and NLP Master Practitioner. She is passionate about the development of individuals and teams and how this contributes to creating long-term organisational growth.

As Managing Director of Dynamic Growth Training (Pty) Ltd, Diane specialises in Performance Improvement solutions for corporate clients, which entails consulting, workshops and coaching.

Diane is currently studying with Access Consciousness and in her own words "My interest and passion is to raise consciousness - mine and others. As this happens we begin to perceive what wasn't available to us before and this literally opens new worlds, new possibilities and new choices". In real terms this is about discovering what it means to become a better human being, partner, friend, sibling, teacher, team member, business owner, leader.... It includes being aware of the impact we have on ourselves and each other, on our environment and other living creatures. It also includes moments of real honesty and awareness around what contribution we make to this world and to discover there is more right with us than we have been led to believe.

Diane is also quick to put new knowledge and insight into practical use such as co-creating coaching or learning interventions with clients. Specifically the qualities of self-leadership & personal mastery are deeply interesting to her, as these are the foundation blocks for supporting others through their transformation. . . "I love exploring what else is possible which includes stretching as a human being and in my everyday work".

Another important quality of being Diane is that of living in congruence with her values and feeling appreciation and gratitude for this life of family, friends, health, yoga, cycling... the list goes on. She loves to travel and has done so in SA as well as to Australia, Bali, Japan, New Zealand, France, Germany, Madeira, New York, California, Mexico, Argentina, Brazil and Mauritius.

Contact details: diane@dgt.co.za www.dgt.co.za

Personal-Intel in the
Age of Transformation

Exponential growth is disrupting everything from the clumsy, old-fashioned systems that used to run the world to our core beliefs. *Warp-speed* shifts are changing the very fabric of how each of us lives life on this planet and progressive leaps forward - once dismissed as 'idealistic' - are now possible.

To give you an indication of how far we've moved, my first book - *EQ: Emotional Intelligence for Everyone* – was written in the late 1990s when telephones were only used for conversation and none of the following terms had been heard of; email, sms, website, Google, Yahoo, blog post, YouTube, wi-fi, ADSL, GPS, Android, Twitter, Facebook, App or WhatsApp and clouds stored nothing but water vapour.

More pertinent though is the progressive leaps in technology that have allowed scientists to take a virtual peek into the human brain. Developments in fMRI scans (functional magnetic resonance imaging) have provided such radically new insights that age-old beliefs about the brain, the mind and human behaviour are being turned on their heads (so to speak).

One of the far-reaching shifts in the field of psychology that has implications for all of us has to do with personality which was considered to be relatively fixed. Now we know the human mind is a collection of habits acquired and reinforced over a lifetime. If our habits are learnt it means they can shift which is great news because presently it is virtually imperative that they do so.

Untold opportunities brought about by tech also mean there is no longer a need for any of us to stay stuck in a dead-end job or outdated career where boredom makes the days seem long enough to make life feel exhausting. Now we can all emulate Madonna—the performer not the virgin—and keep reinventing ourselves even if this means switching careers three, four, or even five times.

Why Personal Intelligence?

The field of 'emotional intelligence' (EQ) has too grown up from its birth in the early 1990s. Daniel Goleman's first book *Emotional Intelligence: Why It Can Matter More than IQ* (1995) spread the word like wild-fire and the matching fervour inflated the role of EQ to lofty heights.

But the truth about EQ's rightful place is there wouldn't be much point in having highly-developed skills in the social and emotional areas if one had little or no rational intelligence (IQ). Without the ability to think, how would these EQ skills help us and what would we use them for? We know the point of developing one's emotional and social skills is to help us think straight and communicate ideas clearly enough to gain co-operation.

Discoveries about the thinking mind demonstrate that thoughts and feelings work in tandem to produce intelligence. These developments led John D. (Jack) Mayer (who, along with Peter Salovey originally coined the term 'emotional intelligence') to use the more encompassing phrase 'personal intelligence'. Personal Intelligence describes the combined workings of EQ + IQ, and Mayer's definition of the new field of personal-intelligence involves reasoning: the ability to reason about ourselves and other people.

On a practical level, personal-intel is about being *future fit* as it requires both rational and emotional intelligence to fathom and navigate a world so refreshingly unrecognisable that it appears almost uncharted. No matter how old we are, the mental and emotional habits we acquired applied to structures that are being disrupted and dismantled, and if we continue to stubbornly resist these shifts, we're likely to collapse along with them.

In a nutshell, being *future fit* is about keeping an open mind which – among other things - means reconditioning the outdated wiring in our thinking brain to entertain some of the more mind-blowing ideas we will encounter.

Systems Overhaul

1) Thoughts: Our personality – or perception of 'who we think we are' - is the sum total of beliefs we absorbed via the 'memes' surrounding our development. Memes are units of social conditioning, which may not necessarily be right or even true; they are simply ideas that gained traction through repetition (via family, community, society) and their influence shouldn't be underestimated.

Memes are powerful and inescapable - everything we think or feel is influenced by memes - including: values, social status, manners, spiritual or religious beliefs (or lack thereof), political affiliations, view of sexual preferences, food choices, brands we prefer, what *not* to wear, language and jargon, stereotypes, choices about movies or TV programs, leisure activities, sports (or teams) we do or don't support, what we consume (both how much and why), attitudes to parents and parenting, reading or education, respect or lack thereof for elders or authority, and the list goes on and on, continuing right down to the more bigoted notions held by some, such as racism and sexism.

The power of memes should never be underestimated. Their influence is so potent that the role of free will in our decision-making processes appears questionable. Memes are ideas we absorbed - much like a sponge absorbs water – making us passive recipients of other people's views. These views had little or nothing to do with who we really are. So who we *think* we are presently is not much more than the sum total of other people's thoughts, ideas or needs about who *they* thought we were or who *they* would like us to have been. And, if such ideas are learnt, the upside is we can uninstall memes that are outdated or those that no longer suit us.

In the book *You Are Not Your Brain: The 4-step Solution for Changing Bad Habits, Ending Unhealthy Thinking, and Taking Control of Your Life,* authors Drs. Jeffrey Schwartz and Rebecca Gladding acknowledge that memes influence the mind, but we can also use our mind to alter this programming. They offer an easy process to deal with obstructive memes such as conservative views (let's say outdated gender roles) or unhelpful beliefs (such as 'I'm not good enough').

I have simplified their 4-step process as follows:

1. **Relabel:** Label these learnt beliefs for what they are: 'memes'. Block these unhelpful thought/s by repeatedly telling yourself; "It's not ME. It's my MEMES!"
2. **Refocus**: Divert your attention to focus on more wholesome ideas or activities and view the thoughts, urges, and impulses for what they are: something to dismiss, not something to focus upon.

2) Emotions: Our emotions run the communication system between the thinking brain and body and the 'traffic' flow between our brain and body produces sensations (good or bad) that we call *feelings*. These feelings originate in our brains but we experience them in our bodies.

Scan your body while recalling the best thing that ever happened to you. Scan your body again while remembering something awful like being fired or getting the boot from a beloved. No doubt the sensations in your body will feel quite different.

I like to think of the emotional system as a complex network of highways and roads between our brain and body. If there are no snarl ups or blockages, the traffic can run freely and we label this sense of flow *happiness*. Being relatively happy most of the time gives us clues about our wellbeing (physically, mentally, emotionally and spiritually) and because 'happiness' is the fuel that moves us forward we call this driver, *motivation*.

The opposite is true of stress. Being stressed tells us all is not well. The traffic is congested or snarling-up rather than flowing. On a physical level the 'traffic' I am talking about literally refers to the flow of chemical messengers from the brain to the body, and these 'messengers' we call *hormones*. Hormones influence our immune system. Uncomfortable feelings – like those associated with stress – make us pay attention and push us to do something about the situation, hopefully, before we get ill.

In an article in the 2015 edition of Psychology Today titled *Beyond Happiness: The Upside of Feeling Down,* writer Matthew Hutson, says; 'Emotions are not inherently positive or negative. They are distinguished by much more than whether they feel good or bad. Beneath the surface, every emotion orchestrates a complex suite of changes in motivation, physiology, attention, perception, beliefs, and behaviors . . . Each component of every emotion has a critical job to do—whether it's preparing us to move toward what we want (anger), urging us to improve our standing (envy), or allowing us to undo a social gaffe (embarrassment).'

Hutson claims we have the wrong idea about emotions. 'They're very rational; they are means to help us achieve goals important to us, tools carved by eons of human experience that work beyond conscious awareness to direct us to where we need to go …. They are instruments of survival; in fact, we would have vanished long ago without them.'

People often label some feelings 'bad' purely because they make us feel bad but it turns out these feelings contain important messages that can help us move forward. I liken 'bad' feelings to the dashboard warning lights in a motorcar. These lights only turn on when something is wrong i.e. our motorcar is not running well. The same thing happens in our brains and bodies. When we feel uncomfortable enough with the situation we're in we will make an effort to change it.

We can minimise the length of time we feel bad by addressing the situation as soon as we notice the discomfort. In the back of my books I have included an 'Emotional Dictionary' to help decode the meaning of feelings but - if you don't have access to this - start by paying attention to whether you feel happy or unhappy. If the answer is 'unhappy' then you will need to dig a little deeper to find out why. Avoid blaming other people – of course some people can be most annoying – but that has more to do with their misery than anything to do with you and blaming them won't help you untangle the chaos in your traffic system.

Instead, try applying some of these questions to life situations that make you feel unhappy:

*What is this feeling telling **me**?*
*What choices have **I** made to get here?*
*Why did **I** make these choices?*
*What's holding **me** back?*
*What are **my** options?*

And here comes the $64k question:
*What benefit am **I** deriving from frequently being in this state?*

The last question is important because science now knows that the mood we regularly experience is the one we will become addicted to – and yes, I do mean the word 'addicted' in the strongest possible terms. Your brain becomes addicted to your mood in the same way as it can become addicted to drugs like heroin.

The sorry part is that your brain doesn't mind (if you'll excuse the pun) whether your moody 'drug-of-choice' favours happiness or unhappiness. But you need to. We know emotions have the power to shift perception and behaviour, to change how focused or motivated we are and they have an effect on our physical health, so it may be worth considering becoming addicted to the state that makes us feel most alive—happiness?

Scientists – like Bruce Lipton who authored the book *The Biology of Belief* – have witnessed that being happy is the best growth promoting substance for our bodies right down to a cellular level. When Lipton talks about 'growth' he isn't referring to our waist or height but rather to the health of our cells. In his research he noticed that cells react to hormones linked to fear and negativity as if they were toxic. Cells are known to move towards nutrition and away from toxins leading Lipton to conclude that we either love life or fear it. Trying to do both at the same time is as absurd as attempting to get your car to reverse while pushing the accelerator.

If you are alive today it is likely you will be overwhelmed by fear. Not only does modern society trigger our alert system frequently enough to make us half-daft (sensationalised news, noise, traffic, speed, crowds, etc.), but this is also continuously ramped up by unrelenting fears that emerge from the deceptive memes that created our insecurities: What if I'm not good enough? What if I lose my job? What if my partner leaves me? Are my kids safe? How am I going to pay for their studies? How will I pay off my debt? Can I afford retirement? What if I'm ill? What if I fail? Left unchecked the fear *blah, blah,* is unremitting.

However, it is worth noting that the only reason we have an emotion called 'fear' is to protect ourselves at the moment our life is being threatened. If this was under threat, feeling afraid will make us act instinctively. Even though media can lead one to believe threats lurk around every corner, carrying high levels of fear cannot protect us from any of life's random events: it just makes us feel unnecessarily hyped-up and anxious, all the time. But, perpetually experiencing such high levels of stress will either make us crazy or ill.

We can tame the fears that haunt us by putting our imagination to good use. Imagine your body is a vessel containing your fear in liquid form – a toxic liquid to be more precise. Find out the level of this liquid: is it at ankle, waist, neck, or forehead height? Now ask yourself 'Is my life being threatened right now?'

If you've got time to ask the question, then the answer must be a big fat *'NO!'*

Most of the time, our fears have nothing to do with a real threat to our life. So it's safe to imagine pulling the plug on this toxic liquid and throwing out those pent-up toxic feelings. If you practice this technique regularly, you will eventually start noticing as soon as fears begin to rise in your system and you'll learn to chuck them out immediately.

Why should you do this? Firstly, fear is the jittery emotion that prevents you from feeling comfortable in your own skin and secondly, by eliminating imaginary fears, you will no longer be vulnerable to other people's manipulation - be they partners, bosses, family, friends or foe.

3. Behaviour: Thoughts and emotions (or – if you prefer - memes and feelings) influence our decisions and decisions guide our behaviour. Although decisions determine your destination, confidence builds competence which in turn builds the steps towards success. The definition of 'success' I work with involves you achieving whatever it is that you want. Obviously, this requires doing the work to discover what is important to you and – contrary to popular belief - it has nothing to do with loving yourself.

Over the past few decades the meteoric rise of the meme promoting self-esteem has convinced many that an unyielding belief in oneself is not only key to success, but also the panacea for all ills. Now that we have experience with a couple of generations raised on the central importance of self-esteem, the proof is in the platitudinous pudding, and it's leaving a bit of a bad taste.

Research psychologists show that the evangelical fervour surrounding self-worth is not just a bad idea; it is dangerous. Instead of producing well-rounded individuals, self-esteem evangelists have wittingly or unwittingly influenced a concerning rise in levels of narcissism which is having a destructive effect on society.

In the book *The Narcissism Epidemic*, researchers Jean Twenge and Keith Campbell claim, 'American culture's focus on self-admiration has caused a flight from reality to the land of grandiose fantasy. We have phony rich people (with interest-only mortgages and piles of debt), phony beauty (with plastic surgery and cosmetic procedures), phony athletes (with performance-enhancing drugs), phony celebrities (via reality TV and YouTube), phony genius students (with grade inflation), a phony national economy (with $11 trillion government debt in 2009), phony feelings of being special among children (with parenting and education focused on self-esteem) and phony friends (with the social networking explosion).'

Adult achievement is built upon developing confidence in your abilities, it is not dependent upon the fake idea of you loving you. Malcolm Gladwell in his book *Outliers: The Story of Success* stated that anyone investing some ten thousand hours of rehearsal in a given field is guaranteed to stand head and shoulders above the crowd.

While this statement may be appealing it is somewhat misleading. The actual research Gladwell is misquoting was done by K. Anders Ericsson, a psychologist at Florida State University, who concluded that 'exceptional performance is a result of about ten thousand hours of *deliberate* practice.' Ericsson's research emphasizes that spending ten thousand hours (that's twenty hours a week for ten *years*) simply repeating the same thing over and over without learning or improvement is unlikely to result in genius or greatness.

Gladwell's version could however explain why some people have developed expert status as a whinger or complainer . . . nevertheless, true greatness results from continuously striving to improve performance in the key skills related to your area of interest—regardless of whether that means building strengths or developing your natural areas of intelligence.

Reality is something psychologist Dr Stephen Briers emphasizes in his book *Pscyhobabble: Exploding the Myths of the Self-Help Generation*. He says that there is seldom concrete evidence for the scientific-sounding claims made by all manner of self-help books including the inflated value of self-esteem and the usual mind-power suspects (positive thinking, the idea of unlimited potential and the emphasis on being blissfully happy *all* the time). He also demolishes delusions that claim we are masters of the universe who have superpowers capable of healing our bodies and controlling our lives.

We know achievement-gurus peddling nonsense about developing a 'millionaire mindset' and the so-called 'law of attraction' can be persuasive. They also get away with it because followers seldom weigh up snake-oil solutions against credible scientific research. And why would you? What's the harm of indulging in a bit of feel-good fantasy, anyway? To a point followers of fancy may be right but what happens when these solutions don't deliver? It's quite simple really. Cerebral snake-oil pushers share tactics with those flogging useless produces in the weight-loss industry. Both claim; if our products don't work for you, you are doing something wrong ... and instead of making consumers raise a sceptical eyebrow they resolve to try harder.

Even so, when you end up still feeling unhappy and are financially a little worse off than you were before (remember these gurus know how to charge) disappointment turns to disillusionment. Inescapably, the feel-good paradox will end up making you feel worse than before you started which is why I recommend real life instead. Philosopher and journalist - Julian Baggini - says the only privilege we have is to control our own growth and he maintains, 'If you think of yourself not as a thing, as such, but as a process, it's actually quite liberating.'

So instead of wasting time and energy on fantasy, do the work, pay attention to your inner world (memes and feelings), focus on what you want and throw everything you've got at making your life work. Nothing can hold you back if you keep yourself 'future fit' and do whatever it takes to be so damn good that no one can ignore you.

Steph Vermeulen

She has been leading pioneer in the field of EQ for almost two decades. Author of the original 1999 best-seller *EQ: Emotional Intelligence for Everyone* she has embraced cutting edge scientific advances that have matured EQ into the now all-encompassing field of **Personal Intelligence**. As a meme-buster who wrestles with the status quo she is a sought after conference speaker and her practical seminars inspire people to participate in what she terms *The Exhilarating Disruptive Revolution*. Steph has also published a book on women's issues - *Kill the Princess* - and her work has changed lives in Southern Africa, Europe, India, the Middle East and the US.

Evolving Through Pain:
Tuning Into Myself

"You cannot prevent the birds of sorrow from flying over your heads, but you can prevent them from building nests in your hair." an old Chinese proverb

It does not matter how many encouraging books we read, motivational talks we hear or well-meaning advice we receive, we are never fully prepared for the impact of losing a loved one. Whether the loss of a loved one is anticipated or not it still takes us by surprise.

The death of my parents within a couple of weeks apart was one of my most difficult experiences. I was daddy's little girl. However, the day of my mom's passing was one of the most transcendent moments of my life. Perhaps it is because she was the last of my parents to go. She died three weeks after my dad. Maybe the pain was most excruciating because she was the mother. Maybe the pain of her death came while I was already grieving that of my father. Anticipating her death, and her actual death, came with a different kind of grief. Though I thought it would be a relief - bringing an end to her suffering- as she had been intermittently been ill for a long time. When hearing the sad news, that shook me up inside. I felt raw, exposed, vulnerable, devoid of answers, unable to understand the mysteries of life. I realised that however the end of a loved one may come, one cannot know just how it will feel, until that moment arrives. It is life changing.

A couple of days after my mom's funeral I went back to work. I could not take more leave days. I had only five days left from my family responsibility leave. I had used many of my leave days when my father died. I continued with my crazy work schedule and I buried my thoughts about the death of my parents in a box to retrieve them at a later stage. I literally tucked it away. At some stage, I learned that my boss called my friend and asked her: "Has Ayanda cried yet? I am worried about her, she is continuing with life as if nothing happened."

My other friends would call and ask "Have you started grieving"?

I would respond "You cannot force it, you cannot say wait a minute now I am going to grieve."

I realised later that I was wrong - you actually can induce it by taking time out to remember your loved ones and allow yourself to be aware of the pain and process your feelings.

Anyway, I immersed myself in my work until one day I had a not-so-good day in the office as one of my colleagues made me very upset. I cried so much and realised that I was not just crying about the fight in the office, I was crying for more, my parents' death. I diverted my emotions from what had made me upset at the office to the fact that I had lost my parents. When parents were alive when I got angry I would call them. They belonged to the generation of the 1920's therefore did not understand the 21st century work dynamics, nevertheless I would call them and hearing their voices would make me feel better. I longed to hear my father asking: "Uphilile ntomb'am" (Are you well my girl). He was able to sense when I was not okay. He would say, "Yhu ndiyakukhumbula ntombi" (Eish I miss you my girl) even though we had spoken a couple of days before. Such wonderful kind of love. Not being able to call them, it started to dawn on me that the next time I visit my parents' place, they would not be there anxiously anticipating my arrival. I thought about how my mom was very proud of me. The last time she heard me speak was at my late brother's memorial lecture. She stood up, weak as she was, and shouted repeatedly "Ntwazana" (my little girl). I began to realise that some of my happy moments are gone, outings with them and my children. I arrived home with big, puffy red eyes. I went to bed early. I tried to sleep but I could not. I had spurts of explosions. The issue is that when my parents died I did not have time to confront the pain as we were all busier with the funeral arrangements than we were with acknowledging our loss.

8 WAYS I PREVENT PAIN FROM "NEST-BUILDING"

There is an old Chinese proverb that says, *"You cannot prevent the birds of sorrow from flying over your heads, but you can prevent them from building nests in your hair."* In other words, even if we deal with loss of different kinds, we can find a way to let them navigate their way through us, and eventually regain our pleasure in life itself. Below is a list of activities that I continue to carry out to avoid "nest-building". Whether planned or unplanned they are surely working for me but because people are different you might find them not suited for you based on your personality and lifestyle. However, it is my hope that the suggested activities may help someone to generate ideas about how to manage feelings of grief.

- Reach out
- Solo travel
- Get still
- Keep a journal
- Dance
- Avoid a big move
- Count blessings
- Stay connected to your spiritual source

Reach out

Coming back to the day I broke down, I cried uncontrollably, and like a baby suffering from colic, I would cry at the same time, every day, while driving from work and going to bed. This lasted for about a week. I was scared of going to bed. I knew what would happen. I felt sorry for my husband who was unable to sleep, trying to comfort me. I cried as if my mirrors were broken. I felt as if a mirror for ME is shattered as I used to see myself in the way my parents saw me and now that they are gone, my image of myself is gone as well. I felt the loss of what my parents saw in me, the loss of a dream, of hope and of what could have been. My mind started going over and over what happened, imagining every detail. I began to think about all the things that my parents said leading to the days of their death. I thought about what those things meant. They counseled us to live as a collective with other members of our external family. The question facing us now was: How will we go on as a family without them? Will we still operate as a unit? Will my eldest brother be able to stay at home and take over the role of my father? Is that not too much to ask? What is going on in his mind? What is he feeling in his heart? Is he not scared of failing in his newly acquired status? Does he not feel insecure around five very strong women who are capable of leading themselves? Does he know that we just want him to be our brother - nothing more, nothing less? Does he know that we will be there for him throughout? What about my other siblings? How are they experiencing their grief? I then felt so overwhelmed to the point of exploding. But one thing about me is that when I don't know something or when I get stuck, I reach out. I did exactly that.

Upon deciding that I needed to take time out, I set up a meeting with my boss to inform him of my situation and the difficulty in adjusting to being back at work as I tended to snap at every little thing and make a mountain out of a molehill. I then wrote to a couple of friends in different Asian countries who I once studied and lived with, to let them know about my situation. My Bhutanese friend told me about the importance of focused breathing when the pain overwhelms me. She said I must count while breathing slowly in and out and empty my thoughts for five minutes. She invited me to visit her and join her on a pilgrimage which included a lot of hiking with a reflective focus as no talking would be allowed. The pilgrimage involved mountain and valley walks as well as visiting beautiful monasteries in remote areas. All three of my friends invited me to visit and stay with them but I took the more familiar one - India – having been there before. Additionally, the Indian invite came with concrete dates that coincided with the Diwali festival as well as a generous offer of a sponsored return flight ticket.

Solo travel

I love solo travelling and strolling through airports because it has been mostly while travelling alone and meeting people outside my genre that I have initially imagined some of the extraordinary things that eventually happened in my life and in the process, I have also discovered some important truths about myself. I spent ten days in India but by the time I left the country I was a different person. The visit gave me hope, inspiration and revived me in just about every way possible. This being my second visit to the overpopulated country, it was not the same as the first as this time since I was at the lowest point of my life. The second visit was full of reflection and reviving moments. I have travelled a lot in my life but India remains the most spiritual country I have ever visited. It is spiritual in the sense that it forces you to deepen your connection with what is truly important to you in life.

Yes the country is chaotic, a bit challenging but it is beautiful and soul-enriching at the same time. To fully enjoy India you have to be adventurous, be a seeker and a person who wants to really see new things out there and experience the world in all its raw and different forms. Every member of my friend's family took turns to pamper me, each offering their portion of trying to reduce my pain. My friend's dad would read me English poems he composed himself, while her brother would cook and I would eat as if it's my last meal. The sister in law would take me shopping and the cousin would preach to me about Osho's concept of the inner and science of awareness. The entire trip made me yearn for life, more life with meaning and purpose.

Get still

Whether too busy or in denial, not acknowledging how we feel prevents us from truly healing ourselves. In my case I buried my thoughts every time they tried to resurface, choosing to push them away by saying my parents were too old, I have so much to do, I have to be strong, I must move on, what happened is part of life. I should instead have had the courage to allow the memories, however painful they were, to rise to the surface of my consciousness and allow myself to truly feel the emotions associated with thoughts about my parents. I learnt that to truly connect with emotions requires a high level of awareness and some degree of effort to put aside regular moments of stillness.

I learned that although awareness is immanent it does not just happen; I had to invite it in, silently and adeptly in the midst of all the chaos taking place around me. To be fully aware of what I really feel in any given moment is not easy as I am always overscheduled, with less time for friends, for family, for community, for taking stock or to just be. However, I realized that unless I form a habit of making time for a moment of stillness, however short-lived, just to reflect on my day before I sleep or first thing when i wake up etc. the world I live in will sap my ability to be fully human. The advice of my Bhutanese friend about the role of deep breathing has become one of the most powerful tools I have ever learned to help me reach a state of stillness, a relaxed and calmer state of mind, to become fully aware of my feelings I also feel that as women especially, we sacrifice so much because of societal expectations and as a result we think about ourselves last.

One of the things that made it hard to talk about how I truly feel with some of my friends and relatives was the response they would give me "but they were very old". This made me feel that my parents' death was less of a loss than if they were younger. I felt judged and that people thought I was ungrateful for all the years they spent with us when other people lose their parents tragically at a young age. People forget that however old they were, they were still my parents and I loved them. While there is no formula to respond or to support someone you care about who is bereaved, for me the most important of all is for people to BE PRESENT by following the bereaved's lead of course. Grief is a very personal experience and belongs entirely to the one experiencing it therefore people should accept that they may not know what to say, and that is okay.

This is the reason I started looking for a more personal self-reflective non-judgemental outlet in the form of a journal. I must confess it's difficult to find time to write; there are many months that went by where I couldn't write a thing, yet when I could write it was one of the main tools that helped me to understand what's really going on inside me. Keeping a regular journaling practice has raised my level of awareness and put me in charge of my healing journey.

Dance

Dancing for me is more than letting off steam as it involves the body, emotion, mind and community. Biodanza and Salsa are the two forms of dance that I got engaged in shortly after returning from India. A South

African friend suggested that I attend Biodanza as she believed it would help me. I found this form of dance transcendental as it led me to an altered state of consciousness and greater control of my feelings. I started the beginners' level of the class and through it I confronted my pain through projecting in it and having a great instructor who is also a medical practitioner and a personal coach was a godsend because it gave me comfort as well as a sense of being in charge of my physical body, feelings and actions. In Biodanza every part of the body moves - even toes are lifted, hips are wiggled, arms are fully stretched and now and again you feel your heart beat, your being present in the moment. The carefully selected music in Biodanza facilitates the understanding of getting in touch with yourself, both physically as well as emotionally and spiritually.

Whatever form of dance that brings awareness of the body, mind and soul, I believe will contribute much to pain management. But, like any medicine related to managing pain, it can be counterindicated, therefore it is important that your dance instructor knows about your situation and understands your needs at any given point for it to yield positive results.

Avoid a big move

Sadly my arrival in Pretoria in 2009 to start a new job coincided with the death of my sister who passed away on my very first day at work. It was very hard as I had not yet created an adequate support structure since it was a new environment altogether. More so because my son, whom I fetched from home after the funeral, began to throw strange tantrums throwing himself backwards on the floor every now and then. I became concerned and called his doctor in East London who said 'listen, people do not realise that moving to a new place is a big change, more so because you just lost your sister, so your son might have sensed sadness at home coupled with the new environment, that's huge for a two year old so give him love and enough time to adjust'. He told me not to take him to any health practitioner but to observe him for about two weeks and then decide what steps to take. Indeed after a week and a half it had stopped, my baby became his bubbly self again.

Immediately after the death of my parents I received a very attractive job offer but I decided not to accept it. This was one of the best decisions

I have ever made in my life. I say this because now and then at the office I would cry for no apparent reason, for example once a colleague delayed to sign an urgent document and I reacted by weeping. My normal self would have confronted him, I would have tried to understand what is taking so long, whether there is anything that he is not happy with etc. I did not do all of that, instead I sobbed. He then responded by giving me a very warm hug. Yes I would have earned more than I do now and all of that, but I realised that I was so vulnerable and needed the comfort provided by colleagues who know me well instead of being in a new job, surrounded by strangers in times of grief

Count blessings

The greatest gift that God has given me is people - friends and family.

It is with gratitude, not self-satisfaction that I say I have been so blessed with the friends that I have in different parts of the world, playing varying roles in my life. In times of my crisis I have always marveled at the way my friends would do anything to reach out to show their love and support and that has sustained me. To know that people care about you when you at your lowest is truly a blessing. Some of my friends ask me what is the secret of attracting so many good people in my life. The other day a friend told me about the concept of synchronicity or "meaningful coincidence" which implies that just as events like bumping into other people who are similar to us may be connected by causality, they may also be connected by meaning. I honestly believe God puts people in our paths because He knows we'll need them.

My family is a special lot. Two of my sisters put their lives on hold for two years and went to stay with our parents until the end of their lives. I can't find words that are strong enough to express how much that means to me and how much I thank them for all they did and showed me.

Stay connected to your Spiritual Source

Whatever your beliefs, staying connected to your Spiritual Source realigns your sense of self to something bigger that you may not ever have imagined was within you. This is the legacy that my parents left us with - the fact that there is in my case as a Christian, a merciful God out there. My parents never went to school and when they used to talk about God they would call him "Umdali" (the Creator) and would say it with such conviction that it would make you feel as if they are talking about a person whose infinite power humans will never understand. When my late brother was in exile, my mom would pray that "Umdali" hides him under His wing, and indeed he came back safely after 12 years. My mother believed and made us believe that in any situation we find ourselves in "ukhona Umdali" (the Creator is present). I am extremely grateful for this spiritual strength as it makes me face each day anticipating new opportunities and always seeing every cloud as having a silver lining. Knowing that there is a spiritual force who created all in life sustains me and makes me maintain inner quiet and strength in the face of challenging and seemingly incomprehensible events. I see every day as another chance and move through the world with confidence bringing all what my parents taught me - our history and heritage as people who paved the way for me.

Ayanda Roji

Ayanda Roji holds a Master's degree in Local and Regional Development from the Institute of Social Studies at The Hague in The Netherlands. She is Heading the Research and Knowledge Management Department at the Johannesburg City Parks and Zoo in South Africa. Ayanda's interest is much concentrated on urban politics and governance. She is passionate about people centred public spaces as such she is a strong advocate of new alternative practices such as co-design that support non-professional forms of knowledge. Ayanda uses her educational background and activist experience, to build bridges between nature, cities and people. She is part of several international research programmes aimed at building accessible, inclusive, environmentally sustainable and safe public spaces. Ayanda loves reading, travelling, thoughtful conversations and discourse about Africa.

Printed in the United States
By Bookmasters